Teach Now!
Modern Foreign Languages

The companion website for this series can be found at **www.routledge.com/cw/teachnow**. All of the useful web links highlighted in the book can be found here, along with additional resources and activities.

Being taught by a great teacher is one of the genuine privileges of life. Teach Now! *is an exciting new series that opens up the secrets of great teachers and, step by step, helps trainees and new recruits to the profession to build the skills and confidence they need to become first-rate classroom practitioners.*

Written by a highly skilled practitioner, this practical, classroom-focused guide contains all the support you need to become a great modern foreign languages teacher. Combining a grounded, modern rationale for learning and teaching with highly practical training approaches, the book guides you through all the different aspects of MFL teaching, offering clear, straightforward advice on classroom practice, lesson planning and working in schools.

Teaching and learning, planning, assessment and behaviour management are all covered in detail, with a host of carefully chosen examples used to demonstrate good practice. There are also chapters on the essentials of the MFL curriculum, pedagogical techniques, strategies to engage students in language learning, and how to succeed in observations and interviews. Throughout the book, there is a great selection of ready-to-use activities, approaches and techniques that will help put you on the fast track to success in the classroom.

Covering everything you need to know, this book is your essential guide as you start your exciting and rewarding career as an outstanding MFL teacher.

Sally Allan is Assistant Head Teacher with responsibility for student achievement at Forest Hall School, Stansted Mountfitchet, UK.

Teach Now!

Series editor: Geoff Barton

Being taught by a great teacher is one of the genuine privileges of life. *Teach Now!* is an exciting new series that opens up the secrets of great teachers and, step by step, helps trainees and new recruits to the profession to build the skills and confidence they need to become first-rate classroom practitioners. The series comprises a core text that explores what every teacher needs to know about essential issues, such as learning, pedagogy, assessment and behaviour management, and subject-specific books that guide the reader through the key components and challenges in teaching individual subjects. Written by expert practitioners, the books in this series combine an under-pinning philosophy of teaching and learning alongside engaging activities, strategies and techniques to ensure success in the classroom.

Titles in the series:

Teach Now! The Essentials of Teaching
Geoff Barton

Teach Now! History
Becoming a Great History Teacher
Mike Gershon

Teach Now! English
Becoming a Great English Teacher
Alex Quigley

Teach Now! Science
The Joy of Teaching Science
Tom Sherrington

Teach Now! Modern Foreign Languages
Becoming a Great Teacher of Modern Foreign Languages
Sally Allan

Teach Now! Mathematics
Becoming a Great Mathematics Teacher
Julia Upton

Teach Now!
Modern Foreign Languages

Becoming a Great Teacher of Modern Foreign Languages

Sally Allan

Routledge
Taylor & Francis Group

LONDON AND NEW YORK

First published 2015
by Routledge
2 Park Square, Milton Park, Abingdon, Oxon OX14 4RN

and by Routledge
711 Third Avenue, New York, NY 10017

Routledge is an imprint of the Taylor & Francis Group, an informa business

© 2015 S. Allan

British Library Cataloguing in Publication Data
A catalogue record for this book is available from the British Library

Library of Congress Cataloging in Publication Data
Allan, Sally.
  Teach now! Modern foreign languages: becoming a great teacher of modern foreign languages/Sally Allan.
  pages cm – Teach now!
  1. Language teachers – Training of. 2. Language teachers – Vocational guidance. 3. Language and languages – Study and teaching. 4. Classroom management. 5. Communication and education. 6. Education, Bilingual. I. Title.
  P53.85.A44 2015
  418.0071 – dc23
  2014017200

ISBN: 978-1-138-01613-2 (hbk)
ISBN: 978-1-138-01614-9 (pbk)
ISBN: 978-1-315-78119-8 (ebk)

Typeset in Celeste and Optima
by Florence Production Ltd, Stoodleigh, Devon, UK

This book is dedicated to Jon and Samuel

Contents

Contents

Tables

Series editor's foreword

What is this series about, and who is it for?

Many of us unashamedly like being teachers.

We shrug off the jibes about being in it for the holidays. We ignore the stereotypes in soap operas, sitcoms, bad films and serious news programmes. We don't feel any need to apologise for what we do, despite a constant and corrosive sense of being undervalued.

We always knew that being criticised was part of the deal.

We aren't defensive. We aren't apologetic. We simply like teaching.

And, whether we still spend the majority of our working week in the classroom, or as senior leaders, we regard the classroom as a sanctuary from the swirling madness beyond the school gates, we think teaching matters.

We think it matters a lot.

And we think that students need more good teachers.

That's where 'Teach Now!' started as a concept. Could we – as a group of teachers and teaching leaders, scattered across England – put together the kind of books we wish we had had when we were embarking on our own journeys into the secret garden of education?

Of course, there were lots of books around then. Nowadays there are even more – books, plus ebooks, blogs and tweets. You can hardly move on the Internet without tripping over another reflection on a lesson that went well or badly, another teacher extolling a particular approach, or dismissing another craze, or moaning about the management.

So we know you don't necessarily think you need us. There are plenty of people out there ready to shovel advice and guidance towards a fledgling teacher.

But we wanted to do something different. We wanted to provide two essential texts that would distil our collective knowledge as teachers and package it in a form that was easy to read, authoritative, re-readable, reassuring and deeply rooted in the day-to-day realities of education as it is – not as a consultant or adviser might depict it.

We are writing, in other words, in the early hours of days when each of us will be teaching classes, taking assemblies, watching lessons, looking at schemes of work and dealing with naughty students – and possibly naughty teachers.

We believe this gives our series a distinctive sense of being grounded in the realities of real schools, the kind of places we each work in every day.

We want to provide a warts-and-all account of how to be a great teacher, but we also each believe that education is an essentially optimistic career.

However grim the news out there, in our classrooms we can weave a kind of magic, given the right conditions and the right behaviour. We can reassure ourselves and the students in front of us that, together, we can make the world better.

And if that seems far-fetched, then you haven't seen enough great teachers.

As Roy Blatchford – himself an exceptional teacher and now the Director of the National Education Trust – says in his list of what great teachers do:

> The best teachers are children at heart
> Sitting in the best lessons, you just don't want to leave.
> (Roy Blatchford, *The 2012 Teachers' Standards in the Classroom*, Sage, 2013)

We want young people to experience more lessons like that – in classrooms where the sense of time is different, where it expands and shrinks as the world beyond the classroom recedes, and where interest and passion and fascination take over; places where, whatever your background, your brain will fire with new experiences, thoughts and ideas; where, whatever your experience so far of the adult world, here, in this classroom, is an adult who cares a lot about something, can communicate it vividly and, in the way she or he talks and behaves, demonstrates a care and interest in you that is remarkable.

We need more classrooms like that and more teachers to take their place within them.

So that's what we have set out to do: to create a series of books that will – if you share our sense of moral purpose – help you to become a great teacher.

You'll have noticed that we expect you to buy two books. We said we were optimistic. That's because we think that being a great teacher has two important dimensions to it. First, you need to know your subject – to really know it.

We know, from very good sources, that the most effective teachers are experts in what they teach. That doesn't mean they know everything about it. In fact, they often fret about how little they feel they truly know. But they are hungry and passionate and eager – and all those other characteristics that define the teachers who inspire us.

So we know that subject knowledge is really important – and not just for teaching older students. It is as important when teaching Year 7s, knowing what you need to teach and what you can, for now, ignore.

We also believe that subject knowledge is much more than a superficial whisk through key dates or key concepts. It's about having a depth of knowledge that allows us to join up ideas, to explore complexity and nuance, to make decisions about what the key building-blocks of learning a subject might be.

Series editor's foreword

Great teachers sense this and, over a number of years, they build their experience and hone their skills. That's why we have developed subject specialist books for English, mathematics, history, modern foreign languages and science. These are the books that will help you to take what you learned on your degree course and to think through how to make that knowledge and those skills powerfully effective in the classroom.

They will take you from principles to practice, from philosophy deep into pedagogy. They will help to show you that any terror you may have about becoming a teacher of a subject is inevitable, and that knowing your stuff, careful planning, informed strategies –all of these will help you to teach now.

Then there's *Teach Now! The Essentials of Teaching*, which is the core text because we also believe that, even if you are the best informed scientist, linguist or mathematician in the universe, this in itself won't make you a great teacher.

That's because great teachers do things that support and supplement their subject knowledge. This is the stuff that the late great educator Michael Marland called the 'craft of the classroom'. It's what the best teachers know and do instinctively, but, to those of us looking on from the outside, or in the earliest stages of a teaching career, can seem mysterious, unattainable, a kind of magic.

It's also the kind of stuff that conventional training may not sufficiently cover.

We're talking about how to open the classroom door, knowing where to stand, knowing what to say to the student who is cheeky, knowing how to survive when you feel, in the darkest of glooms and intimidated by preparation and by marking, that you have made a terrible career choice.

These two texts combined – the subject specialist book and the core book – are designed to help you wherever you are training – in a school or academy or on a PGCE course. Whether you are receiving expert guidance, or it's proving to be more mixed, we hope our ideas, approaches and advice will reassure you and help you to gain in confidence.

We hope we are providing books that you will want to read and re-read as you train, as you take up your first post, and as you finally shrug off the feelings of early insecurity and start to stretch your wings as a fully fledged teacher.

So that's the idea behind the books.

And throughout the writing of them we have been very conscious that – just like us – you have too little time. We have therefore aimed to write in a style that is easy to read, reassuring, occasionally provocative and opinionated. We don't want to be bland: teaching is too important for any of us to wilt under a weight of colourless eduspeak.

That's why we have written in short paragraphs, short chapters, added occasional points for reflection and discussion and comments from trainee and veteran teachers, and aimed throughout to create practical, working guides to help you teach now.

So thanks for choosing to read what we have provided. We would love to hear how your early journey into teaching goes and hope that our series helps you on your way into and through a rewarding and enjoyable career.

Geoff Barton
with Sally Allan, Mike Gershon, Alex Quigley,
Tom Sherrington and Julia Upton
The *Teach Now!* team of authors

Acknowledgements

I'd like to take the opportunity to thank Geoff Barton for asking me, and convincing me, to write this book, as well as for editing it as part of his series.

I would also like to thank my husband and son for their never-ending patience and encouragement during the time I was writing the book.

Thanks also must go to Helen Price, a fellow linguist and head teacher, who supported me as a critical friend and provided the German language input.

Finally, I would like to thank my own French and Italian teachers for providing me with the opportunity and the inspiration to become a modern foreign languages teacher.

Abbreviations

AFL	Assessment for learning
AGT	Able, gifted and talented
CAT	Cognitive ability tests
DBS	Disclosure and barring system (previously CRB)
EAL	English as an additional language
EBacc	English Baccalaureate
FLA	Foreign language assistant
IEP	Individual education plan
ILP	Individual learning plan
KS1	Key Stage 1 (Years 1–2)
KS2	Key Stage 2 (Years 3–6)
KS3	Key Stage 3 (Years 7–9)
KS4	Key Stage 4 (Years 10–11)
KS5	Key Stage 5 (Years 12–13)
MFL	Modern foreign languages
NQT	Newly qualified teacher
SEND	Student with educational needs and disabilities
SOW	Schemes of work
TA	Teaching assistant
TL	Target language

Introduction

Why do you want to be a French teacher? Did you always want to be a French teacher? Why teach French and not something else? You can speak French fluently and you only want to teach?

These are questions that I have been asked several times on different occasions. The decision to become a French teacher was something I did not take lightly; during my training year, I thought it might not be the thing for me. A trip to see my mum in Cornwall during the Easter break, a few long beach walks later and several in-depth conversations with my mum (who is now a retired primary head teacher), the decision was cemented: I wanted to be a French teacher.

My response is the same: Yes, I knew from the age of 11 I wanted to be a teacher; yes, I can speak French and I wouldn't say 'only' teach. I wanted to be a French teacher because I love speaking French; I love France and everything French. I feel like I 'go home' when I arrive on French soil. I've felt like this since I was 16 and experienced my first trip alone to Chamonix, France, and those feelings have grown stronger as I have grown older.

Why did I want to be a French teacher? Because I have a passion for the French language and I want to be the teacher who passes on my passion and enthusiasm for the language. I became enthused by two of my French teachers – Mrs Williams (who was also my form tutor for five years) and Mr Leech. I want to be the teacher who is remembered by my students for having that kind of impact.

I care about young people and I feel strongly that they should have the opportunity to learn as many different languages as they are able to. In an ever-changing world of technology and growing competition for jobs, having a language gives young people the chance to be 'globally mobile' and the opportunity to stand side by side with their European and worldwide counterparts.

During my 15 years of teaching, I have taught French to Years 7–13, GCSE and A level. I have taught Italian to adult learners and to GCSE level. I have also taught German to Year 7 beginners (and a stint to Year 11!). And finally, I am now teaching Spanish to beginners.

In short, why do I teach French? Because I love it. As a student I was asked to write a reflective piece of writing on becoming a language teacher. My piece was one of two from our cohort that was chosen to be published in a language-teaching journal. This was my final paragraph:

> I firmly believe that if you want to teach it is in your blood and that desire never goes away, although it may fade over the years. This year has opened my eyes to that fact. I enjoy teaching and enjoy the challenges that each day brings. Even when things have not been good, I have tried to stay positive, smile and get on with the task in hand.

This book is one of a collection of books aimed at student teachers. Its purpose is to give support and advice to you as a student teacher during those times when you may be questioning whether something is going well, or not so well. It will provide suggestions to different areas of teaching and learning that are pertinent to teaching modern foreign languages (MFL). It is a practical guide that aims to help prepare you to teach languages. There is not one way that is better or more correct than another. However, through certain key principles and priorities, I do believe that you will be able to teach languages confidently.

There are a total of twelve chapters, the first of which starts with looking at the essentials of the curriculum, giving an outline of the key components in teaching languages. The four key skills are addressed, as is the subject of target language.

Chapter 2 moves on to thinking about pedagogy techniques and gives suggestions of what might work best when teaching languages.

Chapter 3 is based around the skill of planning. It takes in turn the differences between long-, medium- and short-term planning. It gives examples of different types of plan and what you need to do and when.

Chapter 4 considers assessment and the variety of ways that you can assess student progress. There are some suggestions of ways to track students using different methods.

Chapter 5 addresses the topic of differentiation and how to ensure that you make your teaching challenging for students, while being supportive to all ability levels.

Chapter 6 explores the use of different types of register and language within the classroom to be able to question, explain and give back feedback effectively.

Chapter 7 discusses different strategies to ensure good behaviour in the languages classroom. There is a strong emphasis here on making language learning relevant to all students and therefore engaging them in their learning.

Chapter 8 continues and digs into the realms of teacher observation and how to deal with observations as a student teacher.

Chapter 9 considers and reflects on the issue of stress and how to deal with the pressure of the job. The topic of work–life balance is also introduced in this chapter.

Chapters 10 and 11 move on to explore the time when you start to think about applying for a job, what to do, and how to prepare for an interview. There are also suggested interview questions in Chapter 11.

Finally, Chapter 12 covers some of the possibilities that you may encounter during your first term in post, how to prepare effectively for it, and how to cope with things such as evening events and parent consultations.

Each chapter finishes with several suggested activities, as well as some suggested talking points to allow you to think about and reflect on the contents of the chapter within your own setting.

Curriculum essentials

1

What are the key components and challenges in teaching this subject?

Target language

Many trainee MFL teachers stress about the question of teaching in the target language (TL). They wonder: What is best practice when it comes to using the TL (the language you are teaching, e.g. French/German/Spanish) in the classroom? How much should you use it? What terms are seen as key language? How much TL should be used?

Many languages teachers have quite strong views on the topic of TL, but I would advise that you have to find your own way and use the amount you feel most comfortable with. I use it as much as it feels natural to do, in particular interacting with students, but I can say that I very rarely use it when introducing a new grammar concept.

There are times during the lesson when it would seem natural to speak to the students in TL. For example:

- greetings at the door as students are entering the classroom;
- farewells at the end of the lesson and leaving the classroom;
- taking a register and expecting a response in the TL;
- giving classroom instructions and establishing routines;
- setting up language tasks or activities, such as reading tasks or a listening activity.

Curriculum essentials

There is an argument that you can teach a whole lesson in the TL, creating an immersion environment and persevering against all the odds in order not to fall back into English.

This can provide its own challenges.

It is obvious that, as a languages teacher, you have to speak the language in the classroom, and you have to encourage students to do the same. You have to experiment with the students you have, depending on their experience to date, and consider what will work best for you in the situation in which you find yourself.

How can you support your students to use the TL?

During one observation, as a student teacher, I remember my tutor drawing up a tally chart against the students in the class and how many of them spoke the TL during the lesson.

I often think back to this and, when I am teaching, I try to keep a mental note of who has spoken French to me during the course of the lesson. It is so easy for some students to sit back and allow the more enthusiastic, more confident students to speak up in the TL.

Often, for targets at parents' evenings, I may set as a target for a quiet, shy student to try and interact at least once with me or another student in the classroom in the TL. Some suggestions to support your students to understand you speaking the target language are as follows:

- using gestures/mimes can help, for example, nodding/shaking your head;
- using visual clues – flashcards or an old overhead projector are a change to a powerpoint/visualizer (ask your head of department if there are any in the department);
- choosing vocabulary that uses cognates or that just sounds similar to English or can link into the topic;
- ensuring that the students understand by asking for a helper/interpreter to check for understanding.

If you are unsure, particularly with your second/third language, there are lists available online and in teacher resources material that will give you an idea of the kind of TL you should try and use in the classroom as a starting point. For example:

- *Ouvrez vos cahiers.*
- *Tournez à la page . . .*
- *Un peu de silence s'il vous plaît.*
- *Quelqu'un veut lire?*
- *Avez-vous fini?*
- *Tout le monde est prêt?*

And you should encourage students to use the TL for real purposes within the classroom. Use classroom displays to support this too. For example,

- *J'ai oublié mon cahier.*
- *Je suis désolé d'être en retard.*
- *Puis-je ouvrir la fenêtre?*
- *Puis-je aller aux toilette?*

Chapter 6 explores in depth the subject of using different types of language when explaining something or using questioning in the classroom. This includes the language that you should use when giving feedback. There is certainly a place for using the TL when marking books too.

The easiest thing for a student in a languages lesson is to say, 'I can't do it', 'I don't speak French', 'I don't understand' or 'I don't get it'. Students can so easily become disengaged and switch off if they are sitting in a classroom trying to listen to a teacher speaking, from their point of view, gobbledegook.

How many times have you tried to do a listening activity, set it up perfectly, explained the task, felt good about it and that all students knew what they had to do, and you began the audio, and students responded, 'eh?', 'What did they say?', 'Can you repeat that bit, Miss?'? It still happens to me, and it is infuriating!

The importance of communication

For years now language teaching has been based on a communicative approach. You are less likely to see more traditional methods such as translation of long paragraphs and class dictation. David Nunan (1991) lists five features of communicative language teaching; these are:

1 an emphasis on learning to communicate through interaction in the target language;

2 the introduction of authentic texts into the learning situation;

3 the provision of opportunities for learners to focus, not only on the language, but also on the learning process itself;

4 an enhancement of the learner's own personal experiences as important contributing elements to classroom learning;

5 an attempt to link classroom language learning with language activities outside the classroom.

The emphasis of this approach is for students to understand a meaning, rather than the form of the language (language structure), and to be able to communicate this meaning effectively so that there is a shared understanding. This means that students and teachers can communicate with one another, using the TL as the focus, and the learners all have something that they can say and also something that they can discover.

Creating a culture within the classroom where the students can, and are willing to, communicate with one another, as well as with you, the teacher, is key. As soon as the students can see the evidence of their own learning, it will build a level of confidence within the students, but also develop more of a 'can-do' approach within the classroom.

There are different ways to develop this kind of culture. One way is to use differentiation, once you have identified your strongest learners in the classroom. You can rely on them to deliver the correct response, and, at the same time, they are demonstrating the language to the weaker learners within the class; children learn as much from listening to one another speaking the language as they can from you.

A second strategy to develop a more communicative style is by using the 'no hands up' approach.

Imagine being in a classroom where students are not allowed to put their hands up, only to ask a question. As the teacher, you are leading the class in their interaction and their learning. If you invite students to put their hands up to answer a question, you invite others to sit back and do nothing by not putting their hands up.

This strategy works really well once you have learned all of their names (or with a seating plan in your hand). You can even ask the students for their responses when you are writing on the board, or sorting the next task. It is a very effective way to ensure that all students are being attentive, all students are listening and all students are prepared to give you an answer.

This means that students cannot hide behind those who are more confident linguists. Earlier in the chapter, I mentioned the concept of all students speaking some TL within the lesson. This approach means that you can ensure that all students participate one way or another within the classroom.

Students quickly get used to this and will therefore expect to be asked to answer in the TL. For those who are incredibly shy or find the language very difficult, I ask for 'helpers' to be able to prompt them if necessary. (There is more on this in the 'speaking' section of the four skill areas below.)

The four skill areas: reading, writing, listening and speaking

The National Curriculum in England dictates the topics that are taught to students in secondary school from the ages of 11 to 14. GCSE specifications continue to do this once students have opted to continue the subject at KS4 (14–16). National Curriculum levels that have been used in the past to report on students' progress and attainment are being removed and are no longer a statutory requirement. There are no current plans to replace them.

In MFL, National Curriculum levels have been a way to demonstrate a stepped approach for the students at KS3, clearly showing where student are succeeding, as well as what they needed to do in terms of developing the four skill areas.

Assessment should continue to be done through the four skill areas, as this will enable students who have particular strengths in listening or speaking, for example, to be able to see where they are succeeding and where they still need to develop.

Over time, languages departments, alongside their school policies, will develop their own systems of assessing the four skill areas to show progression. Assessment continues at KS4 with four papers for the GCSE examination. Students have to demonstrate their ability in reading, writing, listening and speaking by completing four separate papers. Currently, the controlled assessments in speaking and writing make up 60 per cent of the final grade. GCSE reforms are planned from 2015, and so this may alter in time.

When thinking about planning lessons, I still look over the final plan and check that I have enough tasks and activities to cover all four of the skills. I ensure that I include reading, writing, listening and speaking skills in every lesson.

Reading

Getting students to read can be difficult enough in English, never mind in another language. Start small and start early is my advice. As soon as students start learning a foreign language, they should be encouraged to read vocabulary in context.

Reading will develop and broaden vocabulary, as well as contextualize it, using and demonstrating important grammar structures. Reading texts doesn't have to mean reading books. It can start with short sentences. Students may well be daunted by a longer text, so encourage progression by starting early; they can move from single words and short phrases to longer sentences and paragraphs.

In time, students should also be encouraged to read for gist and then to use their understanding to work out the meaning of any unfamiliar language. This will become easier for them as they develop their skills of looking for clues, paired with grammatical knowledge.

Here are twenty suggested reading tasks:

1 newspaper headlines: identifying grammar structures and recognition of vocabulary;
2 newspaper/magazine articles – regional newspapers in France are a lot easier and more accessible for younger students to understand than *Le Monde* or *La Libération*;
3 reading comprehension with questions in English (language content more challenging);
4 reading comprehension with questions in the target language (language content made easier – possibly with multiple choice questions);
5 letters and emails: reading comprehension;
6 using websites for research purposes;
7 reading poetry for vocabulary recognition or consolidation;
8 create a role-play and cut up the sentences, and students must read it and rearrange in the correct order;
9 using novels or parts of fiction to demonstrate a grammar structure, or to stretch abler students or A level students;
10 road signs taken from web pages or own photographs for understanding;
11 TL books at all levels;

12 lists of vocabulary;
13 reading to follow instructions;
14 reading to work out puzzles;
15 reading phrases to sort into parts of speech;
16 reading phrases to sort into different tenses;
17 reading to complete a treasure hunt;
18 reading to dictate to a partner;
19 reading song lyrics while listening to the song;
20 reading blogs.

Writing

Writing in the target language is an important skill for students to be able to communicate, usually more formally, what they want and what they need to say. Students may be more reluctant to write the language, and it may be more difficult to be accurate than in their speaking. However, many students prefer the writing skill, as it is a more individual skill and they don't usually have to do it in front of the class.

There are lots of fun strategies to get students writing in a foreign language, and so, again, start with small steps and progress to the more extended writing that is required towards the end of KS3 and at GCSE level. It does take a lot of practice to become proficient in writing, and students may become frustrated with it, as they may not see a lot of progress or success for chunks of time.

This is where your expertise as a teacher will need to come in to find ways and strategies, from building confidence in your weakest learners to stretching the most able. Students have to start to understand that the more description they can use in their writing, the better they will become, and the more grammar concepts they can 'show off'.

One of the best ways to do this is through modelling the way you would like the students to write. You can also provide scaffolding in the form of writing frames, removing them as the students grow more confident.

Writing is similar to speaking in this detail, and students will need to develop the ability to use the vocabulary and structures that they know and are learning to express what they want to say. In time, they will become independent, and this is to be promoted, but it will take time.

Here are twenty-one suggested writing tasks:

1   responding to a letter or an email;
2   writing postcards;
3   writing poetry, e.g. acrostics for the less able/beginners;
4   labelling drawings or diagrams (single words or phrases);
5   creating cartoon strips;
6   writing a newspaper/magazine article;
7   using exemplar sentences and manipulating them to students' own needs;
8   using a writing frame to support extended writing;
9   writing lists;
10   describing pictures;
11   writing creatively using imagination;
12   writing song lyrics;
13   writing jokes;
14   writing interviews;
15   writing one-word answers on mini-whiteboards;
16   quiz answers;
17   writing a story in a group, one sentence at a time, folding over the paper each time;
18   creating a web page;
19   writing a timetable;

20 creating a survey graph and presenting the results in full sentences;

21 writing a film review.

Listening

It is my opinion that the listening skill is the most difficult one to nurture in young people. It is also the easiest skill for them to dismiss. Students can lack a level of confidence and very easily start to panic, or indeed just switch off altogether. 'I can't do this.' 'I can't understand Spanish.'

It is really important that they concentrate and try to make sense of the language, even though they may not understand every word. Students will 'hear' the language they are studying within a recorded passage, but will they 'listen' to it?

Many young people find it very challenging to identify foreign words, as the speech may be too fast, or it may be a totally different accent to your own. Your students will get used to listening to you, and perhaps a foreign language assistant (FLA).

You can build confidence by speaking in the classroom as much as you can in the TL. You can encourage students to listen to songs in the language and complete gap-fill exercises to develop the art of identifying key words from a topic area or a grammar concept.

You can support the listening by ensuring you have the transcript (if you are not confident enough to repeat it from memory) and repeating the key phrases yourself. It may be appropriate at times to give the students the transcript so they can follow it. You can also ask the students to predict the language they might hear and create a tick list of key terms or phrases that they might hear.

Some learners will grasp the listening activities immediately; others will need support. You will have to weigh up where your students are in terms of the support they will need. This skill needs a lot of practice, and I would suggest that every lesson have an element of completing some type of listening skill-based task.

Here are twenty suggested listening tasks:

1 listen to a weather forecast;
2 listen to order sentences;
3 listen to songs and fill in the gaps;
4 use CD-Roms for listening activities;
5 listen to the radio;
6 listen to podcasts;
7 carry out listening comprehension with questions;
8 listen to interviews;
9 listen to peers/teacher/language assistant;
10 (watch and) listen to the news on the Internet;
11 listen to recognize vocabulary;
12 listen and then write (dictation);
13 watch French films and listen for key grammar concepts or specific vocabulary;
14 listen and repeat new vocabulary;
15 listen to news headlines and match to pictures;
16 listen to example GCSE question papers;
17 listen and translate;
18 listen to and assess others (peer assessment);
19 listen for mistakes;
20 listen, memorize and repeat sentences.

Speaking

Developing students' skill in speaking the language is all about creating the right culture in your classroom. You need to have a culture that is a 'have a go' culture. It doesn't matter if students get things wrong to start with. Use repetition in a way that is non-threatening. Don't highlight to everyone that the sentence may be incorrect. Offer praise for good pronunciation, intonation or having a good accent.

Curriculum essentials

Students have to feel confident to want to speak the target language, either to you or to the other students around them. This needs to start early on too. Teaching vocabulary and asking students to repeat is a good place to start.

One-word answers may be sufficient for real beginners (possibly at primary school), but there is no getting away from the fact that students have to be able to converse and communicate more fluently through KS3 and into KS4.

What you want to try to avoid is students learning large passages of the language off by heart. Sadly, as the controlled assessment at GCSE currently stands, it is more of a test of memory than of knowledge. I like to encourage my students to talk in the language about what they want to talk about, but they need to use the vocabulary that they know.

To be able to speak well in a foreign language, students need to display a certain amount of spontaneity. As a teacher, this is tough to teach. It takes time for students to be spontaneous in their spoken language.

Students find it difficult when they realize that they may not be able to say exactly everything they want to say. They have to remember that they are fluent in English, and it is probably their mother tongue, and so trying to translate word for word is a no-no. They are probably not fluent in the language that they are studying, but they are learning and they are developing. It is frustrating for them. So the key is to teach them how to use the language they know and manipulate it to describe what they want to say.

Also, students sometimes need to get over the barrier of accepting that they may have to 'fib' at times to demonstrate that they can use the language, in order to show that they have made progress. For example, a student may be talking about what they did last weekend:

Qu'est-ce que tu as fait le weekend dernier?

J'ai fait beaucoup de choses. Le samedi, je suis allé(e) au cinéma avec mon copain, Pierre. Nous avons vu un film. C'était génial parce que j'adore les films d'actions. Plus tard, nous avons pris le bus pour aller en ville. Nous sommes allé(e)s au restaurant. J'ai mangé les pâtes avec une sauce tomate. C'était délicieux.

Here, the student has shown that they can:

1 use the past tense correctly, using both regular and irregular forms of the verbs;

2 use an imperfect tense correctly;

3 use the first person verb (*je*) as well as a plural verb form (*nous*) correctly;

4 use two different opinions and justifications.

The student may well have not done these things at the weekend, but has been learning about using the perfect and imperfect tenses together. The student has demonstrated that they can use the tenses correctly and at a good level of language. This develops their confidence. It is a starting point for them to then go on and become a more independent language learner, able to explain other things that they may have done at the weekend.

Most students want to be able to speak in the language. Most students can be encouraged to speak in the language, some as long as they don't have to speak in front of the whole class. Use this to your advantage. Quickly assess who are the big speakers in the class. Who won't mind standing up in front of everyone and demonstrating? Who are the shy students, for whom it would be their worst nightmare to do that? Find ways for all of your students to develop their speaking, in whatever form that may be. Develop their confidence in speaking, and this will undoubtedly develop their speaking skills in the TL.

Here are twenty suggested speaking tasks:

1 describing pictures;
2 role-plays;

COMPANION @ WEBSITE

3 information gap tasks;

4 answering questions about self/others;

5 presentations;

6 recording interviews;

7 repeating songs;

8 repetition in whole class, groups, individuals;

9 discussion;

10 debates;

11 reading out loud;

12 giving instructions to peers;

13 using TL for requests in the classroom;

14 acting out a play;

15 answering the telephone (internal calls only or imaginative) and responding to the caller;

16 hot seating – one student answering other students' questions;

17 finding someone who . . . (*trouvez quelqu'un qui . . .?*): students have to ask other students for information to complete the questions;

18 singing a song;

19 creating and recording a news/weather report;

20 spelling bee.

Teaching and learning of grammar

I am a strong believer that 'grammar is power'. I often tell my students that the more grammar they know and understand, the more powerful they will become.

It is vital that students learn how to learn a language. If they want to continue learning languages, or you want to inspire them to continue with their language studies, the students must learn about how they work. Grammar is almost like the code that they need to crack to have the ability to learn the language; it is like problem-solving.

At KS3, the need to communicate would take precedence over accuracy in the learning process, particularly with complex German grammar. As the students develop their language skills, I would then place more emphasis on accuracy as the communication developed.

I also enjoy teaching grammar structures, because this is when students can most easily demonstrate making progress. You are not only seeing it in front of your own eyes, they are too. It is transparent in terms of progression, and I would advise any teacher to use a grammar concept as a learning objective in a lesson observation.

Students have to learn grammar. There is no escaping that fact. There are lists in the National Curriculum, as well as in any GCSE specification, of grammar structures that need to be taught to the students. However, students have to demonstrate that they understand the concepts and can use them in context. This is assessed through the speaking and writing (the active) skills, whereas, for the listening and reading (the passive) skills, they have to be able to show they can understand and recognize the grammar concepts.

The role of pattern spotting is key in the teaching and learning of grammar. I will always identify the pattern for students (or ask them to spot it, depending on how I choose to teach it). Personally, I also think the role of English and English grammar plays a big part.

During my degree, I spent my year abroad in France as an English assistant in a *collège* and a *lycée*. My most prized possession during this time was my English usage book. It was a new purchase for my adventure in France. By the end of it, it was the most used book from the whole trip.

I learned then, through the teaching of my own language, that it is absolutely vital for the students to understand the grammar concept in their own language before trying to learn the concept in a foreign language.

Curriculum essentials

I go on and on and on about adjectives, nouns, pronouns, verbs, adverbs as parts of speech. I always check that the students understand what I mean (although not so much at KS4). To hammer home this idea, it is a good idea to do a regular, quick question round the class:

- 'What's an adjective?'
- 'What's a verb?'
- 'What's a noun?'

You may be amazed to discover that not all students know the difference. They get confused, and it is a good idea to cross-reference with your English department in your school to check how they ensure the students know and understand parts of speech. Working together to teach students the same thing is a useful and powerful strategy and will reinforce the message that you are both trying to deliver to the students.

My other most popular question in the classroom is 'What's an infinitive?' I ask this question regularly and whenever we are looking at tenses, verb conjugation or any grammar concept linking verbs together. If students are aware of the key terminology from the beginning, it is not something to shy away from, and they will become used to hearing these terms.

Grammar can have a bad reputation, because teaching grammar may seem boring and sometimes uninspiring. Students find it difficult to understand some concepts, but the approach you use to teach grammar can make it a lot more interesting for them. They have to be able to see for themselves how the language works and how it can help and support them to become better language learners.

Inductive grammar teaching: a case study

Inductive grammar teaching is when the students 'notice' the rule and then explain the rule. The teacher gives the students examples of the grammar concept in place, and the students then have the opportunity to work out what the grammar rule is, and how the concept works.

Le futur

Students are given a spectrum on an A3 sheet of paper. On the spectrum there are five sections:

- impossible
- probable
- 50–50
- possible
- certain.

The students are also given an envelope, and in this envelope are ten to fifteen sentences that say something about the future. Here are examples of these sentences:

- *D'ici demain, je serai à Paris.*
- *Ce soir, je mangerai des frites.*
- *La semaine prochaine, je rencontrerai Olly Murs.*
- *L'année prochaine, je passerai mes A levels.*
- *L'Angleterre gagnera la coupe de monde cet été.*
- *Demain, il neigera.*
- *Le weekend prochain, j'irai au cinéma avec mes copains.*

It is important to gather a good mixture of sentences that the students may well be doing in the future, as well as some that most certainly will not happen.

The idea is that the students try to work out the meaning of the sentences using the time expressions and recognizable vocabulary, and they place the sentences in the correct place on the spectrum. It is not really important where they place them at this point, as long as they understand the sentence.

Depending on the ability of the group, you may want to include examples that use all of the parts of the verb and the endings; you may choose to only use the singular versions to start with. You may also want to consider whether you use regular verbs only, or include some irregular verbs to challenge some of the students.

Once they are all placed on the spectrum, you then invite them to look more closely at the sentences and try to discover what the grammar concept is you are exploring in the lesson, and then what are the patterns that are visible.

In groups, the students then need to create the rule for this grammar concept. At this point, they could create a poster to illustrate how they would explain this concept to a younger learner of French.

Deductive grammar teaching: a case study

This approach is a lot more of a teacher-centred approach to grammar learning. The teacher teaches the concept, and then the students practise this rule.

Le comparatif

The teacher may use PowerPoint or interactive-whiteboard software to create a teaching aid for this concept. Students will see examples of how to compare two different things in the language, the teacher making sure to highlight how the adjective changes depending on the nouns that are being compared.

The students will then have some examples to manipulate, changing the language where necessary to make sentences, as directed by the teacher.

The students may then have to compare two school subjects, or two people in the class, or two methods of transport, using the concept.

Active versus passive learning

You may be asking the question, what are active and passive learning? When teaching languages, both styles of learning are very important. Active learning is when the students are very much involved with the learning; it is learning by doing. It is a process where the students are active participants in the learning itself.

With languages, many students will learn more deeply if they are involved in active learning. This means that, whereas it may be easier for you as the teacher to stand at the front of the classroom and deliver the lesson, it is more beneficial to take time to plan activities for the students to run independently, as this will undoubtedly support their learning. This may well mean that students work together in pairs or groups. It will be the interaction between them that will bring about the learning.

Examples of active learning could be:

- class discussions;
- think, pair, share;
- student debates;
- role-play
- information gap exercises in pairs;
- dictation exercises.

Passive learning is what students do as they are hearing, seeing and reading the language. Students do this and learn as they process the language through these skills. Throughout the whole lesson, in fact, they will be, at some point, engaging in passive learning.

Making it 'real'

One of the first pieces of advice I heard from a fellow languages teacher was to make sure I made the language 'real'. What did that mean? I found it tough to understand exactly what this person was saying. How can you make language 'real' within the confinements of a classroom? Yes, there are trips and the position where they sit within students' learning, but not all schools offer them, and not all students can afford to go. Student exchanges are becoming a thing of the past, as parents became more wary of sending their children off to stay in strangers' homes abroad.

However, there is a growing trend of post-16 students going abroad to participate in a week or more of work experience. This is a really good opportunity for them to visit and stay in the country and also use the language for real-life purposes. There are organizations in this country that arrange placements.

The Internet also makes it much easier to bring the language and the culture into the classroom now. Websites such as YouTube can provide a much-needed opportunity to see how life is in Paris or Berlin or Barcelona.

Bringing a language to life, or making it real, can be achieved in a variety of ways. Students need to be able to experience times when they are using the language for real purposes. You can use cross-curricular opportunities here, with drama or music, to bring out more creative language. You can set up a French café on open evening. Within the classroom itself, activities such as information gap exercises can ensure that students are using the language for real purposes.

By using these kinds of activity, students are using the language to gather information that they need to complete the exercise. Role-plays are also a good activity to practise 'real-life' situations.

If you are lucky enough to have an FLA in your school, use them to create situations. Ask the assistant to come into your class and introduce him- or herself. Ask the students to prepare some questions for them.

Vocabulary acquisition

You cannot get away from the fact that the students have to learn vocabulary, and learn it off by heart. It is how they do it that is the minefield. You need to try different ways to encourage the students to learn vocabulary.

A lead lesson (the first of a series on a topic, e.g. 'school') would always have a collection of key vocabulary. You might use PowerPoint, or a piece of interactive software, which may be linked to their course book. You might even use flashcards.

Flashcards are cards with pictures on them and usually have the word on the other side. All languages teachers used them prolifically before the dawn of the interactive whiteboard. They are a really useful and fun resource. Students like them, because they can touch them and hold them up. I would like to suggest that there might be a good collection of flashcards hidden away in cupboards in a lot of modern foreign languages departments. If you find some, use them – they are good fun. You can, of course, make your own, with card, pictures and a laminator.

Here are ideas of different ways to use flashcards:

- Hold up the picture, say the word and have the class repeat the word. Nine cards are enough for students to learn at one time.
- Play noughts and crosses in two groups, using a grid system and sticking the flashcards on the wall in the grid system.
- After introducing a set of cards, hold them in a pile against your body, concealing the top card. Ask the students to guess which card it is that you are hiding. Once someone has guessed correctly, you can either give the set of cards over to the students, or start again with you holding the set of cards.
- Stick a set of cards on the wall. Two students stand at the cards. You (or another student) say a word, and the students have to touch the correct card.

> • Give a selection of cards per table or group. As you shout out the word, the students have to find the picture in their pile and hold it up.

Repetition is the way to ensure that students pronounce the words correctly too, preferably before they see how the word is spelled, to avoid poor pronunciation. Students should also learn the gender with the piece of vocabulary. When they learn that moon is '*lune*' in French, they should learn it as '*la lune*'.

I do not believe that giving students lists of vocabulary with the English translation actually helps them. I think it is a huge waste of resources. Yes, of course, give them a list and use it as a matching activity, with the English in the incorrect order.

For many years, at the beginning of the topic at GCSE level, I would diligently create and distribute more than 100 words in French for my students to learn. I would only provide them with the French (taken from the GCSE specification), and they had to complete the English side. We would check the words together to ensure they had understood and got the correct translation. I would then ask them to learn the words for a test the following week, usually fifty at a time.

For conscientious students, this worked pretty well. Students would learn them and they would also have the lists for reference. However, for students who found French more challenging, or were not so conscientious, this strategy did not work. I had to find different ways to accommodate all of the students in the class, not just those who would go home and quite happily learn fifty words of new vocabulary.

I hear myself every year telling the Year 11 students, 'The reading and listening exams will be won and lost on your knowledge of vocabulary'. Every year, I set the same target for similar students: learn your vocabulary thoroughly and on a regular basis. Encourage your students to keep their vocabulary notes separate from their other bookwork, or, at least, to highlight it and to copy it into a vocabulary book or on to file paper and file it in a folder.

Creating a 'can-do' classroom environment

If you think you can, you can.

All students can learn a language. It is not out of anyone's reach. Yes, certainly, it is more difficult and challenging for some students, but then so could be learning a musical instrument or learning the periodic table.

However, it is the easiest thing for students to say, 'I can't'. How can you create a 'can-do' classroom environment? It is about encouragement and being positive in a lot of different ways. As I have mentioned previously, positive praise could be through commenting on good pronunciation or good use of vocabulary. It could be through saying a student has used a grammar point really well. Some students respond really well to stickers or merits or house points – do promote the school's policy on rewards, whatever it chooses to use.

Consistency will help you as a teacher, and students will respond well to what they know. If students can see that they are doing things well, no matter how small, and they can see that they can do something, that culture of learning will grow. Try not to single out students who you know are very shy, or to 'force' students to speak out loud in front of the class if it will make them feel humiliated (that would be the last time that they would contribute to the lesson).

So, what if a student is getting it all wrong? There must be something positive that you can pick out, and it is up to you to find it and highlight it.

Developing a 'have-a-go' culture

The 'have-a-go' culture goes hand in hand with the 'can-do' environment. Once students see that they will be rewarded for having a go and be praised for lots of different things, they will continue to respond to you.

Students need to know that they do not have to always get it perfectly right to feel like they have succeeded. If they 'have a go', you as their teacher will reward them in your own way.

TALKING POINTS

1 Consider how you will include the four skill areas into your lesson planning. Does it have to be explicit every time?

2 How much TL do you feel comfortable with? What is your expectation of how much TL the students will use in your classroom?

3 How can you support the use of TL in your classroom through display?

4 How can you make language learning 'real' for your students?

5 What do you want your classroom to look like, and what kind of culture will you promote in your classroom?

6 Look back over the suggested activities throughout this chapter and think about how you could develop these ideas within your planning.

Pedagogy essentials

2 What techniques and strategies work best in teaching this subject?

Interaction

Interaction within the languages classroom is absolutely vital to promote effective learning. It will tend to take place teacher to student or student to student. It can be built upon in a stepped approach, so that spoken interaction moves from teacher to student, demonstrating with an abler student in the class (good use of differentiation), to the students using the model provided by you to create their own parts of interaction. Getting the student to be the 'teacher' can also create more interesting interactions.

Exchanges that take place may be primarily using the TL through speaking and asking for responses. These exchanges can be simple, using question and answer, or they can be more complex, expecting the students to ask the questions back to the teacher. Either way, interactions are about building the length of conversation and being able to hold the language and respond somewhat on the spot.

Pair work

This is an essential part of teaching languages. Students feel safer when they are talking in pairs. They have to get used to, and feel confident about, the language in a more reassuring environment.

Pedagogy essentials

Pair work gives them this opportunity. The task needs to have some relevance to the work that you are doing in the classroom and it needs to be achievable. At times you will choose the pairs, but there may be times when the students can choose their pairs.

A set dialogue is the way to start and to gain your own confidence in setting up the task. You may want to model the conversation, or it may be a listening activity that demonstrates the conversation. Either way, once the students have seen or heard the dialogue, it then becomes their turn to have a go at it. You can give the instructions in the TL, keeping it really simple. For example: '*Vous allez travailler à deux. Personne A va demander les questions. Personne B va répondre aux questions. Allez-y. Vous avez trois minutes.*'

This is the easiest way to ensure that students are working together in pairs. Once you are confident with that, you can ask the students to be a little more independent, having to create a conversation, working in a situation that you give them, for example, *chez le médecin* or *à la banque*. Students can be given the parameters to the expected conversation, and then they can work within these parameters.

Once the students become even more confident, and this may work better with GCSE students, you can introduce pictures to stimulate a conversation. There may be a question attached, such as '*Qu'est-ce tu as fait ce weekend?*', followed by a selection of pictures that the students choose at random. This will really help to encourage more spontaneous conversation.

Pair work is really important and is key to practising the language in what some students would feel is a more secure environment for them. However, this does not mean that it has to be restricted to set dialogues. The GCSE speaking examination is no longer based around role-plays, as it has been in the past. Students have to show that they can talk with spontaneity, and there are lots of ways to practise this in the classroom with some of the suggestions above.

Group work

Group work can mean anything from three students working together to even half a class working together, depending on the size of your classes. Group work promotes more independent learning, as well as providing opportunities for peer assessment. You can arrange your groups any way you wish to. In a mixed-ability group, you may choose to group them in ability groups. You may allow the students to choose their own groups. They could have *rouge* and *vert* groups for extension tasks. Group work can allow for a wide variety of types of task, as well as different ways to organize the class. This is also a great way to use any teaching assistants (TAs) that may be in your classroom, supporting the students.

Teacher-led learning

There will always be parts of a language lesson that will need to be teacher-led. Languages are not the same as other subjects in terms of students being able to 'teach themselves'. Just try to set your first cover lesson for a language lesson, when you are out of school, and someone else (not a language specialist) has to take the lesson. It is incredibly difficult. So, traditionally, lessons may well begin with teacher-led tasks, or will certainly have them at some point. You are the expert, and the students are there to learn from you. That doesn't mean that the lessons have to be you, as the teacher, standing at the front, delivering the 'lesson'. It also doesn't mean that the lesson has to be delivered in a 'death-by-PowerPoint' kind of fashion! If you are going to use PowerPoint, then try to limit yourself to a small number of slides. Use other things to make the lesson more interactive – look back at the section in Chapter 1 on flashcards. Try different ways to impart your knowledge to your students.

Student-led learning

Lessons should also have times in them that are student-led. This is one way to use differentiation in the classroom, inviting perhaps your ablest students to teach other students. It could be set as homework to prepare part of the lesson. You could incorporate this as a group-work task. Each student from group A has to teach another student from group B a grammar concept, for example, and then vice versa. Students have to be given the initiative to develop their own knowledge in a more independent fashion. This is not always easy in languages, and it is not always obvious how to do it. If you wanted to, you could do it across the year groups. Ask Year 10 or 11 students to video something they would like to teach Year 7 students as a learning strategy for all involved.

Carousel: planning a 'skills-based' lesson

A carousel lesson takes a lot of planning, but is worth every minute! When you create resources, you must file them so that you can make planning a carousel an easier and quicker task the next time. You will need to consider how many students are in your class and how many students you will want to be in the groups. I would also suggest that you have on the whiteboard the names of who is in each group – think carefully about which students you put together. Is it a good idea to group in ability or by mixed ability? Once you have chosen your groups, you need to create the same amount of tasks; for example, six groups mean you need six different tasks (see Table 2.1).

Tables should be arranged with numbers clearly visible, with an activity task sheet for instructions and perhaps the answer sheet for the students to self-/peer assess. Instructions for the carousel should be made explicit; for example, there are six tasks and 10 minutes per task. After 10 minutes, you need to alert the students that it is time to change activity. You many want to give them a 2-minute warning if they want to assess the task.

Table 2.1 Arranging a carousel lesson

	Listening	Reading	IWB activity	Writing	Speaking (with FLA)	Running dictation
Group 1	1	2	3	4	5	6
Group 2	6	1	2	3	4	5
Group 3	5	6	1	2	3	4
Group 4	4	5	6	1	2	3
Group 5	3	4	5	6	1	2
Group 6	2	3	4	5	6	1

The lesson objective for a carousel lends itself very much to a revision type of lesson, perhaps for a GCSE class, or an end-of-term lesson. It is ideal to bring together a module of work, or a topic, using all the vocabulary and grammar structures that have been used over the course of several weeks or months. Some suggestions for tasks are listed below.

TASK 1: LISTENING

This necessitates having headphones attached to whatever machine(s) you are using to play the listening passage. It might be that your department has a 'Coomber', which is used in many MFL departments. They usually have up to six headphone sockets that can be used at the same time. Otherwise, it may be that your room has several computers, or the school has laptops you can book. Whatever you choose, each student must have a set of headphones and be able to listen to the passage without disturbing the other tasks around the room. This is an individual task, one that students should complete by themselves. They need to have a comprehension task, or a sample GCSE examination exercise. You can also leave the answer sheet available so that they can peer assess one another.

TASK 2: READING

Similar to the listening task, students will need a passage to read and questions to answer. Again, making the answer sheet available allows the students to assess themselves independently from you. This task should be done in silence, and on an individual basis.

TASK 3: INTERACTIVE WHITEBOARD

This is normally the loudest of the tasks, and where you should ideally base yourself. The students will need an interactive task/game/quiz to complete. If your school subscribes to a website such as linguascope.com, this is ideal to choose activities where students can compete within the group against one another.

TASK 4: WRITING

The outcome of this task must be some form of writing in the TL. This can be differentiated, and writing frames or gap fills may be appropriate to use, depending on your students. It could be an extended piece of work, with an instruction sheet listing what must be included, in terms of content as well as grammar structures. You could easily adapt a written activity from a textbook, if you are short of ideas. If you choose to do this, I would advise you to make it your own – so don't just photocopy the book!

TASK 5: SPEAKING (WITH FLA)

If you have a language assistant in the department, this is an ideal opportunity to use him or her. The assistant can take these students out to do small-group work in a different room, or in a nearby corridor. Ensure that it is still on the same topic as the rest of the tasks. If you do not have an assistant, you will need to provide a role-play-type activity or an information gap task (see the Speaking section in Chapter 1). Remember, the task needs to last for 10 minutes.

TASK 6: RUNNING DICTATION

This is probably one of my favourite activities for the classroom, and one that works well in a carousel lesson. The students need to have quite a bit of space in the room for this. Split the group into pairs. One of the pair (A) will need to sit at a desk with a plain sheet of paper. The other (B) will have to find a written passage that is stuck on the wall, far enough away from A to be able to walk to and from the written passage. Person B has to go to the written passage, read some of it and then return to Person A and dictate what they have just read. Person A then has to write it down. This continues until they have completed the passage. I always use two short paragraphs, so that they have a natural time to swap roles. This is an active and fast-moving task. My students have always really enjoyed it.

Carousel lessons are a lot of fun and can be quite noisy, hence having to keep some activities silent. As a student teacher, you may want to ask the normal classroom teacher to be available, or even to act as the language assistant. I would also add that you need to know your class pretty well to be able to plan the tasks to match your students, but also to group the students effectively in order for the tasks to work. You don't want to be thinking about behaviour management during this kind of fast-moving lesson, when your eyes and ears need to be watching and listening to as many of the students as you can.

Finally, it is worth it. You need to try one out to see for yourself how, when you plan it well, the effort is worth it. Good luck. Go for it.

Use of technology: ICT, interactive whiteboard, Internet, social media

For student teachers in today's culture of technology, the issue is not whether to use it or not to use it, it is how to use it, when and how much to use it. Technology is forever changing and developing. My students undoubtedly know how to use my interactive whiteboard better than I do. If I can't do something on the board, or it is not working, one of the students can always sort it out for me.

Whether you have a 'SMART' board, or an interactive whiteboard, with other software, you will have to be able to demonstrate that you can use it efficiently and without much difficulty. If this poses a problem, it is imperative that you ask for support from other colleagues within your department, or help from the IT support department within the school. Any problems that you may encounter could be specific to the board that you have within the classroom, or the software that is running on it. It is better to ask within your school for this support.

Many course books now have their own 'Active' software, which runs alongside their books. Most of them also have the feature of students being able to have their own log-ins, and the possibility to set homework for students to complete at home; there is usually a cost attached to this. It is worth investigating this to see whether it would be cost effective. I have always found them a very useful add-on, especially for A level students.

 The Internet has huge potential to bring your classroom alive. There is a plethora of websites devoted to language learning; most of them are free, but some have a subscription cost. A good place to start is the BBC website, www.bbc.co.uk/languages. There are a wide variety of online exercises as well as videos to watch.

The Internet can bring to life towns that you might be studying, or even just mentioning in passing. The website www.national geographic.com is also a fantastic resource to share images of the towns, cities and countries that you may study. As the Internet is so vast, it is all about taking the time to search and have a look around to see what is useful for you.

Podcasts are also rapidly developing, and these can be listened to on students' mp3 players. They can support student revision very effectively. They can also help students to practise their listening skills. Students will quickly pick up a wider range of vocabulary by listening to a French/German/Spanish radio station's weekly podcast on a regular basis.

Social media have exploded in the last few years, and the majority of teachers, departments and schools are embracing them within their classrooms and establishments. Twitter and Facebook can be very important and powerful marketing tools for a school, as well as a fantastic portal for communication between teachers and students, and teachers and parents. For example, if you are involved in a trip, you could have a Twitter feed so that parents can follow the events of the trip. They can be useful for the resources that your students should be using – articles to read, new clips to watch, any pieces of interesting media, all of which would be in the TL.

You should also find out what the social media policy is within your school, and whether they are something that other departments are partaking in. There is nothing to stop you setting up social-media resources, but you will need permission from your head of department, and maybe permission from someone in the leadership team. The rationale needs to be very clear as to why you would use a Twitter account or a Facebook group page, what it would be used for, who would update it, and who it would be aimed at. There is a lot of scope here, but it may have to be approached in the right way, depending on the school.

Sites such as Pinterest and other sharing sites can also be a very useful tool for collecting and sharing resources. Again, this would need further discussion with your head of department.

Understanding the complexities of grammar

Grammar can be a daunting prospect for a languages teacher. It is vital that you know and understand the different parts of speech. What is a verb? What is a noun? What is an adjective? It is vital, because all of your students who come in and out of your classroom also have to know! Whether you support that learning through displays or regular/constant/consistent questioning, that is up to you. However, the same thing remains: you have to know the answers to those questions. If you are unsure, you will need to remind yourself! At the very least, you will need to know and be able to define (this is not an exhaustive list):

- a verb – and the different tenses that the verbs are to be taught in;
- an adjective;
- an article (definite and indefinite);
- a noun;
- a pronoun;
- a possessive pronoun;
- an adverb;

- a superlative;
- a comparative;
- the imperative.

The best thing to do is check a grammar list from one of the GCSE specifications (or A level specification, if you are teaching A level). Once you are aware of all of the grammar expectations that Year 11/13 have to reach, you can plan accordingly.

It is also a really good idea to talk with the English department and/or the literacy coordinator in the school, to ensure that you are delivering a consistent message when it comes to teaching grammar. A grammar check list is also an effective tool for students, so that they can tick off the parts of grammar that they know (and can recognize) or that they have included in a piece of writing. This can be used from beginner level through to Year 13 and A2 level.

The role of translation

The information that is coming through from the present government (in December 2013) is that students will be expected to develop the skill of translating when learning a foreign language within the new curriculum. This sits very well next to understanding grammar and parts of speech. The majority of students like to try to translate word for word from their mother tongue, probably English, to the foreign language that they are learning. This is not always possible. It is important that the students develop an awareness that you cannot always translate word for word, and sometimes it is more effective if you translate the whole phrase.

Google Translate (or any other online translation provider) is your worst nightmare. If the students are going to use it, and they will, your best bet is to discover its advantages and disadvantages in the classroom together. I have often used wordreference.com, as it is a site that expands the translation. For example, if it is a verb that is being translated, then the site will conjugate the verb for the student to see. It is not just a direct translation. Students need to see the traps of these translation websites, and you can show them. However, if they are supported and shown how to use them effectively, then you can suggest that they use the one that you feel is the most appropriate. Students think that they can use these sites and that you, as the teacher, will not be able to tell.

It is naïve to think that students will not want to, or will not try to, translate the foreign language in any way that they can, and it is your role to support them to be able to do that. Translation has its place in the classroom, and it is not something that should be introduced at AS level.

Using the dictionary and developing dictionary skills

This is a good point to warn you that you mustn't ever assume that your students know things that you would presume them to know! It may sound a bit strange, but, like telling the time, or knowing their 'rights' from their 'lefts' when teaching directions, you should also not assume that your students know how to use a dictionary. I have seen students many times looking for a French word in the English section, and vice versa. I have also seen some students start at the beginning of the dictionary and look conscientiously through all of the letters to look for a word that may begin with a P. The questions you will field may well sound like this:

> 'Miss/Sir . . . this dictionary is rubbish, it doesn't have "is" in it.'

> 'Miss/Sir . . . why doesn't this dictionary have "got" in it?'

You will also see examples of poor dictionary usage in written language. For example:

- *Je manger.*
- *Nous avoir.*
- *Ils tomber.*

And, perhaps worse:

- *Je mange des frites prep mon frère.*

These are all examples with evidence to show that students are not using their dictionaries in the correct way. Students love dictionaries – they think that all of the answers are in them, and that they will make their lives easier.

A dictionary is a fantastic tool, and all languages classrooms should have enough bilingual dictionaries for students to be able to help themselves to them when they need to. Monolingual dictionaries also have a place, especially for abler students and post-16 students. It is really important that students are encouraged to use dictionaries to help and support their learning experience and enhance their development into more independent language learners.

Currently, at KS3, students have to be able to demonstrate that they can find out the meaning of unfamiliar words in order to achieve Level 4. This means using a dictionary effectively. This has to be part of your teaching and planned into the lesson at the appropriate time in the curriculum. In many textbook resources that are available, there are dictionary tasks that you can use to develop dictionary skills. This is a great starting point, but you must remember to remind students to use the dictionary at other times too, in order not to fall into the dictionary traps!

You may also have to remind students how the bilingual dictionary works – two sections, with grammar help possibly in the middle. It is a good idea to identify the abbreviations together and talk about what they mean. If you are feeling brave (you may have studied a module at university), you could also develop something to support the learning of the phonetic symbols, with a link to the correct pronunciation.

Using a dictionary is unavoidably linked with the teaching and learning of grammar and its complexities. If you are consolidating skills in dictionary use, it is a good time to link it with grammar structures too.

ACTIVITIES

1 Can you list the parts of speech that you feel comfortable with and a definition? Can you list parts of speech you feel less confident with and then research the definition to use with your students?

2 Plan a lesson for dictionary skills. Decide which words would be useful for the students to find the translation to. Group the students into pairs if necessary, but ensure that there are enough dictionaries in the class so that all students can see and be involved in learning to use the dictionary.

3 Plan an ICT lesson so that you and your students can discover the advantages and the pitfalls of using the Internet in the TL. Give students help sheets if necessary, to support their learning. Decide what would be the objective of the lesson first before booking an ICT room.

4 Develop a useful website wall within your classroom, so that students can share their ideas with other classes.

TALKING POINTS

1 Consider the ways that you can incorporate the skills of translation from the TL to English, as well as the other way round. How can students learn to develop this skill? When would it be the best time to start developing translation skills?

2 How can the use of a bilingual dictionary support the ablest students, as well as those students with learning needs?

3 How much technology is a sufficient amount to use,
   without taking away from the pedagogy of the lesson? At
   what point does technology become overwhelming in
   the classroom?
4 How can social media be used as a learning tool within
   the languages classroom?

Planning essentials

3

What does good long-, medium- and short-term planning look like?

When you start to plan your own lessons, where do you start? Do you look at the objectives of the lesson that you want to achieve? Do you think about it as a series of lessons, perhaps two or three lessons, to teach a topic area or a grammar structure?

Is it important to consider the half-termly plan or term-long plan? Does your department have an overview of what each class or year group is set to achieve over the course of the year?

A long time ago, my dad taught me the phrase, '*Perfect preparation prevents poor performance*'. This is very true in many senses, but, most of all, it is very true in the classroom. If you are adequately prepared for your lesson, and it is well planned, you will be able to deliver a good lesson. Yes, you will need to be flexible and, in time, when you have grown in confidence, you will be able to identify when a task may not be working as well as you had hoped, and you can change it during the lesson.

Good planning is vital is all senses – long-, medium- and short-term planning. I will show you how I have planned some individual lessons, a series of lessons, a term of lessons and a year of lessons.

When planning your lesson, you also have to consider all of the factors that might be out of your control. For example, the weather may well affect your lesson. I know it may be hard to believe, but windy weather turns what are normally fantastically well-behaved students into ones that you might not recognize.

What time of the day is the lesson? Is it the first lesson of Monday morning or the last lesson on a Friday afternoon? Is it before lunch or after lunch? All of these things might well affect how your lesson will proceed, even if you have planned it well. You have to be flexible to deal with the unpredictable. When is the best time to teach a new grammar concept, and when is it better to teach a topic-based lesson?

You will have had some time to observe other teachers' lessons within your school. Note how lessons may differ according to the time of the day. Try and see the same teacher with the same class, but at different times in the day.

Long-term planning

Long-term planning is all about being able to see the bigger picture in terms of progress. You should be able to see what the students are learning year on year, and how their learning will be consolidated over time.

In some respects, language learning is cyclical: students will learn some of the same things over and over. This may be a grammar structure that they will first encounter in Year 7, be taught in Year 8 and then use time and time again throughout their language lessons. Take the present tense as an example. I can remember teaching sixth-form revision classes, starting with how to conjugate regular -er verbs in the present tense. Students learn this in Year 7. Grammar structures are regularly revisited, but the context will change.

It is essential that you, as the students' teacher, are aware of what has come beforehand, what you are expected to teach, and then what will come afterwards. What are you expected to cover in the academic year, or the key stage?

For those students who start secondary school in Year 7, it is really important to know what they have been taught in primary school. It is part of the KS2 curriculum (Years 3–6) that children have a foreign language provision. Therefore, the department you are working in should have some primary links with the feeder schools. It may well be possible for you to visit and observe some Year 5 or 6 lessons. There is a whole realm of possibilities for primary liaison, and this is worth considering later on.

The new Primary Curriculum for September 2014 now officially states that all KS2 children (Years 3–6) must learn a language. Therefore, gone are the days when you start from scratch in Year 7. It will have an impact in the secondary classroom, and so you need to ascertain what level of language the new Year 7 will have before they arrive in your classroom, in order to plan effectively.

Textbooks are probably the best place to start. They are written with a stepped approach to learning. Most textbooks have frameworks or overviews that come with the textbooks. However, they need to be personalized to your department and to your students. All schools are different, with different intakes and cohorts of children.

Once the long-term planning is firmly in place, it makes the medium- and short-term planning a lot easier and more straightforward.

For example, this academic year, I am rewriting all of the KS3 Spanish schemes of work. It is a huge task, but one that is really important and will impact on my lesson planning in the weeks to come. So, where do I start?

Key stage and yearly overviews

Here is an example:

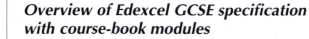

YEAR 10–11, FRENCH, 2013–15

Overview of Edexcel GCSE specification with course-book modules

Personal information, Modules 1 & 2, Year 10, Sept.–Dec.:

- general interests;
- leisure activities;
- family and friends;
- lifestyle (healthy eating and exercise).

Out and about, Modules 3 & 7, Year 10, Jan.–May:

- visitor information;
- basic weather;
- local amenities;
- accommodation.

Customer service and transactions, Modules 8 & 9, Year 11, Dec.–Apr.:

- public transport;
- directions;
- cafés and restaurants;
- shops;
- dealing with problems.

Future plans, education and work, Modules 5 & 6, Year 10, June–July, Sept.–Nov.:

- basic language of the Internet;
- simple job advertisements;
- simple job applications and CV;
- school and college;
- work and work experience.

Controlled assessments

- May–June 2014: writing/speaking;
- Oct.–Nov. 2014: writing/speaking;
- Feb.–Mar. 2015: if necessary.

Each of the year groups (7–9) has a yearly overview of what I will need to cover with them and what they will need to learn. I have also created a key stage plan to ensure that I can cover the whole of the KS3 and 4 courses in the time that is allocated to us. Alongside the KS3 coordinator for French, we have to ensure that students make sufficient progress in order for them to be able to step up to the KS4 curriculum and the GCSE course.

We also want to ensure that all of the students will come away from those three years of languages teaching with a good amount of knowledge and transferable skills, if they choose not to continue with their languages studies at GCSE level. These may include more details such as key vocabulary, possible grammar structures and suggestions for extension work and/or support.

Here is another example, of a 1-year overview for Year 7 Spanish:

MFL DEPARTMENT – SPANISH

Year 7 Spanish, topics overview, 2013–14

Unit 1: *¡Vamos!* (Sept.–Nov.):
- Chapter 1: *¡Hola!*
  –introducing yourself;
  –understanding Spanish pronunciation.
- Chapter 2: *¿Cuàntos años tienes?*
  –counting up to 15;

-using the verb *tener* to give your age.
- Chapter 3: *Feliz cumpleaños*
  -counting up to 31';
  -saying when your birthday is.
- Chapter 4: *Hablamos español*
  -learning about Spanish-speaking countries;
  -understanding regular *-ir* verbs.
- Chapter 5: *En mi mochila*
  -learning the Spanish alphabet;
  -using the indefinite article (*un/una*).
- Chapter 6: *En clase*
  -talking about the classroom;
  -understanding the definite article (*el/la*).

Unit 2: *En el instituto* (Nov.–Jan.):
- Chapter 1: *¿Qué estudias?*
  -talking about your school subjects;
  -using the *–ar* verb *estudiar* (to study).
- Chapter 2: *¿Qué haces en clase?*
  -saying what you do in lessons;
  -understanding regular *-ar*, *-er*, and *-ir* verbs.
- Chapter 3: *Los profesores*
  -talking about your teachers;
  -using adjectives that end in *o/a*.
- Chapter 4: *Me gusta el español*
  -giving opinions and reasons;
  -understanding all adjectival agreements.
- Chapter 5: *¿Qué comes?*
  -talking about snacks;
  -counting up to 100.

Unit 3: *Mi familia* (Feb.–Apr.):
- Chapter 1: *¿Tienes hermanos?*
  -talking about your family;
  -using *tener* (to have).

Planning essentials

- Chapter 2: *¿Tienes animales?*
  –talking about your pets;
  –making colours agree with nouns.
- Chapter 3: *¿Cómo eres?*
  –talking about your appearance and character;
  –using the verb *ser* (to be).
- Chapter 4: *Tengo los ojos azules*
  –talking about eye and hair colour;
  –using adjectives after nouns.
- Chapter 5: *¿Cómo es?*
  –using *tener* and *ser* in the he/she form;
  –using texts as a model for creative writing.

Unit 4: *En casa* (May–July):
- Chapter 1: *Vivimos en Europa*
  –describing where you live;
  –adding extra detail into sentences.
- Chapter 2: *¿Cómo es tu casa?*
  –talking about your home;
  –writing a longer passage.
- Chapter 3: *¿Qué haces?*
  –talking about activities you do in your home;
  –using stem-changing verbs.
- Chapter 4: *En mi dormitorio*
  –describing your bedroom;
  –using prepositions.
- Chapter 5: *Mi rutina diaria*
  –talking about your daily routine;
  –using reflexive verbs.

Medium-term planning

Medium-term planning is what is sometimes referred to as the scheme of work. This should be provided for you as soon as you arrive in the department. If you do not possess or have not seen a scheme of work, please ask your head of department if there is one for you to use.

It should be a working document and not something that is completed and then filed away in a cabinet somewhere. It also should be something to which everyone contributes. This could be an ongoing process, but it is really important that the members of the department feel like they have played a part in the development of the schemes of work.

I prefer to use weekly plans for my medium-term planning and I tend to revise these on a termly basis, depending on how much I have covered with my classes. I also like to collect feedback from my colleagues, to ensure that, when they are updated, changes can be made accordingly.

Either way, these documents should contain the same types of detail:

- title of the unit/topic area;
- a time scale for how long it will take;
- possible learning objectives for the unit/time period;
- vocabulary key to the topic area;
- resources available within the department or shared area on the IT system;
- space for differentiated material (SEND, AGT, EAL) – extension/support;
- any assessment details or requirements;
- possible more generic skills to develop in the unit/topic (literacy/numeracy/ICT skills).

Planning essentials

If you are in a situation where there are no schemes of work, hopefully this will provide you with a starting point and an example of a simple way to start thinking about planning a series of lessons, for a term or more.

Weekly plans

Table 3.1 is an example of a Year 11 half-termly plan.

I choose to create a weekly plan for each of my classes, which covers the whole of the academic year. This is also a time-consuming exercise, but one that will ensure that the class has enough time to cover the entire curriculum.

Weekly plans are not set in stone. They are flexible plans to ensure consistency across groups. They will reflect the balance of the curriculum, as well as outline the expectations of all department staff, and support all staff in their teaching. If you share a class, this is also a very good way of making sure that both teachers are covering their own fair share, and that the students will make the progress that they need to within the year. It also provides a way to deliver the course consistently.

They are a guide to show what topics or grammar structures should be taught and when is the most appropriate time. They also give the chance to plan well in advance, if there are assessment periods in the calendar, or if data are being collected at particular times of the year. You can then plan in your assessments and revision around this.

I remember vividly turning up to my first A level history class and my teacher, Mr Hedley, telling us he had planned all of our lessons for the whole year. I couldn't believe it. I thought he was bananas. I often think about this when I am planning for a whole year. It makes sense to me, and I do it too. It allows you to think forwards as well as reflect on what went well when you come to update the plan the following year.

Table 3.1 Year 11 weekly plan, autumn term

Week beginning	Lesson	Grammar	Assessment
2: 24 Sept.	Speaking preparation for presentation on 'Ma ville'		Vocab test: Ma maison
1: 1 Oct.	Past papers' reading & listening questions/assessments on Module 3 topic of Où j'habite New vocab lists to be distributed for Module 4: Allons-y Module 4, food vocabulary pp 68–9 Using quantities Clothes vocabulary	Partitive article	Individual speaking presentations
2: 8 Oct.	pp 70–1, Making plans Checking vocab lists Revisiting the past tense	The future tense Revise past tense	
1: 15 Oct.	Past tense with être pp 72–3, at the train station pp 74–5, talking about buying clothes	Conditional tense	Vocab tests: clothes & food shopping, writing in the past tense using avoir and être together
2: 22 Oct.	pp 76–7, using the imperfect tense using avoir and être	Imperfect tense	Using present, perfect and imperfect together

1: 5 Nov.	Module 7: tourism pp 124–5, using *aller* Accommodation pp 126–7, weather Vocabulary for holidays	Past, present and future tenses together	Past papers' reading & listening questions on Module 4 topics
2: 12 Nov.	pp 128–9, hotels and travelling pp 130–1, making holiday plans	Comparatives and superlatives Future and conditional tense	
1: 19 Nov.	pp 132–3, describing a holiday pp 134–5, problems on holidays	Using the perfect infinitive	Vocab tests
2: 26 Nov.	pp 136–7, eating out pp 138–9, describing a past holiday (2)	Conditional tense Pluperfect	
1: 3 Dec.	Module 8: *Mode de vie*; food; parts of the body; vocabulary lists for parts of the body		
2: 10 Dec.	Talking about what is wrong with you, ailments, healthy lifestyle, drugs and dependence	Use of '*avoir*' terms Past paper questions on healthy living	Vocab tests
1: 17 Dec.	Module 5: education vocab lists: school, school uniform, times, talking about schools Describing a school day, school rules, talking about future plans	Using several tenses together Future tenses Imperatives *Il faut*	

Day planner: using a teacher's planner to plan a series of lessons

When I was a student teacher, we were not given a planner, and so I decided to make my own. As a result, when I have had the privilege of supporting a student teacher, I always provide them with a planner. First, you need to have some notes in front of you to guide you through the lesson (if you haven't got a full lesson plan), and, second, it is important to be able to refer back to it or remind yourself you need to set homework or collect in the books.

The planner also gives you the chance to see a series of lessons more clearly. If you are given a target of planning a series of five 50-minute lessons to cover the perfect tense, you need to consider how you will do that, and how each lesson will move on to the next one.

Lesson planning

Once you have all of the above in place (and you may well be in a department that does not have all of the above), you can work out clearly where your individual lesson sits within the bigger picture. Where are you in the year? Which term is it? What date is it? Where should the students be in terms of their knowledge? What has come before, and what should be coming afterwards?

Remember you are an individual, and there isn't a foolproof way to plan an outstanding lesson. We all plan differently. This is about you finding the best way for you.

You may well choose to develop your own lesson plan pro forma, use a school one or perhaps an e-pro forma. This type can be helpful in terms of your being able to pre-populate elements of the plan. Try different ways of writing your lesson plan and choose the best way for you.

Start with your lesson objective:

- What do you want the students to learn during the lesson?

Planning essentials

- What progress will they make in terms of knowledge or skills within your lesson?

- How will you ensure that all students make excellent progress?

- How is a language lesson different to plan than other lessons?

- What has come before, and what will come afterwards?

It is an individual task, but all lessons need to be planned according to the medium- or long-term plan of the department.

Decide if your lesson is grammar based or topic based. Decide if it is a lesson where there will be new language acquisition, or whether it is a consolidation lesson. It may be an assessment lesson. Whichever type of lesson it is, you need to decide on your lesson objectives.

Some examples of languages lesson objectives when teaching the future tense could be:

- to recognize the future tense and give some examples;

- to understand fully how the future tense is conjugated in all regular verbs;

- to identify irregular verbs in the future tense;

- to apply the future tense in an extended piece of writing.

It is important for the students to know what their lesson objectives are, but it is not always necessary to display them at the beginning of the lesson. It may be more appropriate to have a starter activity that engages the students immediately on their arrival in the class. The students may even be able to have a guess at what the objective might be, once they have completed the starter activity. It is important to use different techniques, so that the students do not rely on you to tell them what the objectives of the lesson might be.

You may want to include a question that is based on a key concept or skill, e.g. how is the future tense formed?

It may also be an appropriate time to differentiate by outcome for different ability groups within your class; different objectives will show evidence of working at different National Curriculum levels or GCSE tiers/grades. You could also use 'all/most/some' to differentiate the objectives. For example:

- All will be able to recognize the future tense and give some examples.

- Most will be able to understand fully how the future tense is conjugated in all regular verbs.

- Some will be able to identify irregular verbs in the future tense.

Once you have observed some lessons, you will be able to see what is being done by others in the school, and then you can try out some yourself to see what is the best fit for you, and what you want your students to learn.

There are many different pro forma around to plan a lesson. Your school may have its own that you will be expected to use, or you could develop your own.

Once you have decided what you want your students to have achieved at the end of the lesson, it is a case of planning the journey that they will take to get there. What kinds of activity do you want to include? Will you include all four skills (reading, writing, speaking and listening)?

Each task should be linked to the objective(s) and should show progression through the lesson. The tasks should also link to one another in a stepped approach to the learning. The activities should support the learning for the following activity, and so on.

Starters

Your students should be engaged within the first few minutes of the lesson. You may have to complete a register, which obviously has to be done first. However, in your planning, make sure that your students are not sitting and waiting for the lesson to begin.

Planning essentials

Try putting tasks on the desks, so that, as they arrive, the students are immediately engaged in something. This could be a reading task, a puzzle of some kind or some sentences using a grammar concept you are planning on teaching them in that lesson.

Starters should be short tasks that draw students into the objective of the lesson. They could also be tasks that build upon or check their prior learning.

You may prefer the students to come into the lesson and complete the starter task in silence, so that you can complete the register. Whatever your expectations are, make sure they are clear to the students.

Setting homework

You may find there is a homework timetable that you must adhere to within your school. Find out when you are expected to set homework for your students. This will also need to be planned, as part of your lesson planning.

Make sure that the homework is relevant and meaningful. There is nothing worse than homework being set for the sake of it. In one of the departments I have worked in, there was a policy that we would set one 'learning' homework a fortnight. Therefore, I would need to plan that into the series of lessons to ensure that I followed that policy.

There is nothing wrong either with giving students a choice of homework, depending on their strengths. Be aware that not all students will have a computer or access to the Internet. If you set homework that entails using either of these, ensure that the students have time to be able to use the school facilities if they need to.

Another strategy is to set homework in preparation for the following lesson. Students may have to research something, or find examples of language structures. Make sure, however, that you then plan into the lesson the way you will use the homework.

Organizing/sharing resources

You will undoubtedly create a wealth of resources during your time as a student teacher. You will also need to think carefully about how to organize those resources. I still have a big box that has followed me from school to school, and classroom to classroom, which carries in it resources dating back to my student teacher days.

This is the time when you will be trying out lots of different methods of teaching and using different resources. Make sure you keep hard copies of these things in a folder (or a box). It is easy to forget, several years on, what you created to teach 'booking a room in a hotel' to Year 10 students.

You may also want to share resources or try other people's ideas. There are many websites now where other teachers upload their resources and you can download them for free. The *Times Educational Supplement* website is one place to start.

ACTIVITIES

1   Take the time to have a go at creating a weekly plan for one of your classes. Use the example as a template and see if you can make it work for you. Complete a half-term at a time and see if you can gauge the timing of the lessons with what the students are learning.

2   Use some time to complete some student questionnaires to find out what types of activity they prefer to complete, and how well they think they learn as a result. Use your findings to compare them either with activities you do in the classroom or ones that you observe. Do the students learn as well as they perceive with their favoured types of task?

3   Create a bank of starter activities that will engage your students as soon as they come into your classroom.

4   Plan a series of lessons so that you can see for yourself how you build on prior learning.

TALKING POINTS

1   Discuss the value of homework. What is its purpose? As a teacher, why do you set homework, and how do you ensure that it is valuable to the students and their learning?

2   How do you organize resources? Can you share resources within the team you work with? Can you create resources that can be used with more than one language?

3   How can you develop your planning so that you are efficient with your time and can still deliver a lesson that meets all of the required criteria?

4   What happens when students miss lessons through absence, music lessons, sports fixtures, external examinations? Is it your responsibility to enable the student to 'catch up', or is it theirs? What can you put into place for students who have a planned absence? Or for those who are persistently absent?

4

Assessment essentials

Different ways of assessing students' progress (formative and summative)

Assessment is a complex beast in languages. First, there are four skills to assess. How often should you assess? Is there a school policy of regular assessment that correlates with the data collection? Is there an expectation of assessing at the end of each half-term? This needs to be found out first and will impact on your long-, medium- and short-term planning.

In terms of languages, I will outline what it means to assess. I will give some examples of what the relevant terms mean when it comes to languages and some possible suggestions of how to go about assessment.

Difference between summative and formative assessment

- Formative assessment is assessment *for* learning.
- Summative assessment is assessment *of* learning.

Those two very small words change the emphasis of what you're assessing, how you assess and why you assess.

Summative assessment is assessing the students at the end of a block of work, such as an end-of-unit test. You are assessing what they have learned.

Formative assessment involves getting feedback from the students on their own progress and then acting upon it.

It is important to get the right balance with assessment in languages. Some students may feel they are 'tested' all the time. By achieving a balance between the two types of assessment, formative and summative, you will be able to create the right approach to supporting your students to improve and make sustained progress.

Understanding this terminology will support you in the best and most varied ways to assess students. Teachers all regularly assess in a whole realm of different ways. It is because of this that we can plan more effectively.

So, what should assessment look like in the languages classroom?

Assessing the four skills: summative assessment

For many years, assessment has taken place on the basis of one of the four skills: reading, writing, listening or speaking. Often, if I am doing an end-of-unit test, I will make sure I test one passive skill (listening or reading) and one active skill (writing or speaking). Sometimes, there is not enough time to test all four skills every time, so this helps to give a balance.

One of the reasons behind this is as a result of the way the National Curriculum levels have been organized, as well as the natural progression through to GCSE level, where the four skills are also examined in this way.

There is also an assessment scheme called the Languages Ladder, which the National Strategy for England introduced in 2002. Your school may use it in place of the National Curriculum levels, as these are being phased out. This moves from 'breakthrough' at Level 1 through to 'mastery' at Level 17. The first seven levels equate roughly to the National Curriculum levels.

Because four different skills are being tested, it has to be decided at which point you would confirm that a student is working at a level 5. Would the student have to meet all the criteria across the four skills to be assessed at level 5? Would two or three out of the four suffice? This is usually a departmentally agreed area.

However, I will say that it often comes down to a dose of professional judgement and a case of which is the best fit for the student. As long you keep detailed records (written or electronic mark books), you will be able to track your students through the levels and through the skills. In this way, you will also be able to judge which are their strongest areas and their weakest ones.

If in doubt, the majority of course books (especially at KS3) will have clear marking criteria for their textbook exercises as well as end-of-unit tests, and these are linked to the National Curriculum levels. Even though the current government (December 2013) is getting rid of these levels, they are a good starting place, if your school has not devised any other way of measuring progress.

Assessment for learning: formative assessment

Assessment for learning (AFL) is something that should be well embedded in many schools. It was introduced several years ago, and students are now much more involved in their own assessment, either through self-assessment or peer assessment (assessing one another).

It was suggested that research had shown that students learn best when they know what they are trying to learn and the expectations of what they are learning, when they are given suggestions on how to improve on their learning, and when they are involved in assessing each other in order to improve.

As a result, individual subjects undertook a huge re-evaluation of their own assessment structure, relooking at schemes of work and lesson planning to incorporate this AFL.

It sits well within languages, as it provides opportunities to have focused discussions about the criteria that are required to reach, attain or surpass target levels or grades; it allows discussion on types of structure and language that are needed to produce a good piece of work.

In addition, the design of learning through spoken language allows the development of peer assessment, as students listen to one another and can critique each other through peer presentations or dialogues.

There are a huge variety of resources available on the Internet in terms of AFL in languages. You may find that there are resources in place that are used in the department that you are working in. Your head of department may have certain requirements for all students, and how they should be assessing themselves or their peers.

One simple way to start is to use a target-setting sheet in the students' exercise books, where they can record their target grades or levels, and where they can record on a regular basis (every six weeks, per unit or per term) personal targets to improve on their current grade or level. This obviously will depend on the system of student tracking that is used within your school.

You could also develop a student pro forma in the form of a tick list, if students are to peer assess presentations or dialogues. Depending on the criteria, whether it is Year 7 beginners or Year 11 GCSE students, students can tick off items and then give feedback to each other.

Dedicated improvement and reflective time

It is important to give students reflection time as well, once they have been peer assessed, or build it into the self-assessment opportunities. In addition to this, when you return student work or books to them, allow 5 minutes of reflective time for the students to read through your comments.

Closing the gap

'Closing the gap' is a term used to describe activities where students are given the opportunity to improve their work that you have already marked and assessed. For example, you may set your students an extended written piece of writing to assess their ability to reach a level 5 in Year 8. In order to achieve this, they must include more than one tense. If you have come to the end of teaching the future tense, you could set an open-ended task with suggestions of what it may include, which would also have to be the future tense.

If students hand in the piece of work and they have not included the tense you had covered, and are, therefore, only able to reach a high level 4, you would give them that feedback.

Closing-the-gap activities are also completed in green pen. The students are, therefore, very aware that, once they have the green pen (it's a good idea to have a box of them in your classroom), it is the time to improve on their own work, following the feedback.

You collect it in again and re-mark it, highlighting whether they have managed to 'close the gap'. This can also be done by peer assessment, as long as all of the students have the criteria available to them.

Diagnostic assessment

This is an area that you develop more as you teach more. It is possible to make a judgement very quickly as to how good a student is at the language that they are learning. For example, in an interview lesson situation, I would always start with a quick 5 minutes of speaking work, asking personal information on names, age, where they live, hobbies, maybe adding in a question in the past and/or future tense. This way you can ascertain which students are the strongest and most confident in the class.

I would start most lessons with some form of spoken dialogue, whether it is from teacher to student or from student to student, as it allows you to gather information on their prior learning and how much the students can remember from the previous lesson(s).

It is a quick and simple way to assess the students and to work out very quickly which areas need to be developed and which students are struggling in certain areas.

Ongoing assessment

A language lends itself very easily to assessment of students on an ongoing basis. Some students might think that they are being assessed or under the spotlight almost all of the time in their language lesson, and they wouldn't be far wrong. Whether it is an assessment of their speaking ability, or of their ability to comprehend what is being said by you or by another student, you can assess easily and regularly.

Speaking can also be assessed through pair work, or just by your moving around the classroom during an activity and listening to the interactions of the students.

Student tracking

At some point, preferably as soon as you start to teach your students, you will need to start tracking their progress. Your school may have decided to subscribe to an online, web-based program into which you will upload your marks. At the school where I teach, we do exactly that and each department area is able to create its own bespoke mark books to match its needs.

If this is the case, then you will need some training on how to use it and probably log-in details. Once you have these, you will be able to access students' data and be able to upload your own marks. These are very useful tools to be able to use.

However, if your school does not have a centralized scheme such as this, where you enter your data into a school-based system, I would suggest that you might need to create some mark books for yourself. This can be easily done with an Excel spreadsheet, or, if you prefer to follow a more traditional route, you can use the mark-book sheets in your teacher planner. You may want to ask other members of your department what they are doing, or what is expected across the school.

You will need to collect evidence of your assessments somewhere, and this will also include marking, AFL information, summative assessments and ongoing assessments. You may be asked to show evidence of how you know a student is working at a B grade, or a level 6. Also, using data of this kind at parents' evening can be a powerful tool to show the child's progress throughout the term or year.

Marking

The topic of marking could be added to several different chapters in this book. Marking is necessary. You cannot rely on ongoing assessment, or AFL or summative assessment. There is nothing that can replace the regular marking of classwork and homework. Students' work needs to be recognized by you as being valuable. Homework has to be collected in (and sanctions must be put in place for those who fail to do the homework), and it has to be marked and fed back on to make it valuable and meaningful.

At the beginning of each year, I produce my own timetable of when I set homework – there may be a school homework timetable for this, and this must be adhered to – when I collect in homework, and, finally, when the homework is returned. This is my personal timetable for me to ensure that I keep on top of the workload and the marking.

I also keep a record of when I have collected in books and marked sections of work or extended pieces of writing. Again, this can be collected in your mark book or teacher planner.

Student progress is most evident in their exercise books. You can ascertain very quickly a student who is learning effectively, making good progress, and a student who is not.

Perhaps most importantly, marking is also about feedback. As a teacher, you have to give praise and encourage, but also highlight where students are getting things wrong. However, you need to be able to give feedback as to how the student can improve on their work. This is also a big part of AFL. As already stated, students also need time to reflect on this feedback and perhaps complete a green-pen closing-the-gap task.

Assessment essentials

The last step in this process is for the following time that you mark the book, or check the student's work, when you must try and check that the feedback has been acted upon. Have they remembered to include the auxiliary verb when using the past tense? Have they added in the accents on the nouns? Have they corrected their spelling of a key word?

All this is vital to be able to assess effectively your students and their progress, but also to be able to plan more effectively too.

ACTIVITIES

1   Design a tracking sheet for one or more of your classes; it could be one KS3 and one KS4 class. Consider what you need to track in order to identify which students are making expected progress and which students are not.

2   Design an end-of-unit assessment test. Think about what you are testing for? What do you want the students to demonstrate, to ensure that they have effectively learned during the unit?

TALKING POINTS

1   Consider the reasons why we assess students. How can we measure progress? Are there any other ways than to continually assess the students?

2   How important are prior data when assessing the students?

3   Is it possible to demonstrate that the students have made progress without assessment?

4   How often should teachers mark students' books? What should we mark for? What kind of feedback should we provide to the students, and in what form?

Differentiating

5

How to make the subject relevant, challenging and accessible to all ability levels

For many students, learning a language is a difficult concept to comprehend, and it is sometimes easier to fail rather than apply the extra effort that it takes for some individuals to succeed. The key word here is 'individual'. All students are different, and they have different learning needs.

This is where the subject of differentiation has to be addressed. It is imperative that, during the planning of your lessons, you provide opportunities for all of your students to access the curriculum. This can be done in a variety of ways.

Differentiation by outcome is where the students all have the same task, but the expectation of what they achieve is dependent on their individual level of learning.

Differentiation by task is where you provide a variety of activities and pitch the tasks at the level of the students in the class. You may well have between six and ten different tasks going on, although the content covered will be on the same lesson objective.

This comes down to the different groups of students that you will have in your class and your school.

Native speakers

In languages, you may have the novelty of teaching students in your class who are native speakers. This can be either fantastic or scary.

Differentiating

The native-speaking student can be very useful in the classroom. They can help other students or work independently (with you supporting), allowing them to continue to use their native tongue.

They can also easily be encouraged to take their language examination early. If you do not speak their language and they would like to take a GCSE, you would need to consult your head of department, who would then source a linguist to deliver the speaking assessment.

This year, I supported a Year 10 student through his Italian GCSE examination. He is fluent, as it is the language spoken at home, in his Italian family. Although I was able to support him easily through the reading and listening papers, and have an understanding to guide him through the writing assessment, I needed to ask for someone to administer the speaking controlled assessment. I was not confident enough in the language to provide him with the opportunities to stretch him to achieve an A*, which was his potential. I am pleased to say that he did achieve an A*, and I was able to sit in on the speaking exam and assess him on the marking criteria.

It can be scary if there is a native linguist in your class and you are teaching perhaps your second language. In the past, I have taught Italian, German and now Spanish. My degree was in French, and so this is the main language that I can teach. I will only teach the others at KS3 level (Years 7–9). I am quite at ease with a French native speaker in the class and have, in the past, asked their advice sometimes, when I was not 100 per cent sure about something.

However, if it is the case that the native speaker turns out to be native in a language where you are not so confident, there needs to be a conversation with your head of department to discuss further how you can (as a department) support this student. You may well find there is another teacher who is more confident in their language who would be happy to help.

Personally, if I had this situation in my department, I would look for ways to support you in terms of withdrawing the student for some lessons, and perhaps then creating a programme of using the student to support you in speaking activities in the class, in a similar way to an FLA. I would also suggest this would need permission from parents too.

English as an additional language (EAL) students

All native-speaker students also come under the group of EAL students. Within your school, there should be someone who has the responsibility for these students. Therefore, if you have a student in your class who is a native speaker (of a language that you teach or do not teach), they are eligible for extra support.

These students may well be allocated withdrawal time. It may be appropriate for those students to be withdrawn during your lesson. This is a decision that is made according to timetables and availability. However, there would be no harm in asking, if you felt that it would be more beneficial to them to have support in other areas of the curriculum, in the place of trying to learn another language, particularly if their English was very weak.

However, some EAL students can really thrive in MFL lessons, as they are suddenly on a level playing field with the other students. This can only help to develop their language skills and help them learn English too.

As an example, we had a Year 8 mid-year-entry student join the school, who was Polish. She spoke hardly any English and had not learned Spanish or French beforehand. The teacher in charge of EAL (who happens to be in the MFL department) suggested that she use some of her support time to take her out of my Spanish lesson, but with her remaining in the French lesson, in order to provide her with extra English support lessons.

It is difficult to give a definitive answer on strategies to support EAL students, as it depends on their native language and if it is taught in your school. It also depends on the student's level of English and their academic level.

Differentiating

Supporting EAL students is also a school-wide strategy, and so I would also suggest that you find out who is responsible for EAL provision. A good place to start is learning support for advice, if they are not based within the languages department.

Students with educational needs and disabilities (SENDs)

An interesting question to reflect upon is whether SENDs should be learning a foreign language, if they are unable to access the curriculum in English, owing to low levels of literacy. Many schools choose to withdraw some students from their languages lessons to concentrate on supporting these students.

If this is not the case in your school, and you find yourself teaching students who have a low level of literacy, this is where the expertise of differentiation will needed to be applied. You may be teaching mixed-ability groups, or groups that are set by ability. In either case, you will need to plan accordingly to pitch the learning at the right level.

In my opinion, all students should have the opportunity to learn another language. I don't always agree with withdrawing students from my lesson. This is because I believe that it is possible to pitch the learning at the correct level.

All students have to make progress from their individual starting points. This is key with SENDs, as their starting point will probably be considerably lower than that of other students. You will need to know each of your SENDs and their individual needs.

These students may have a statement – meaning that the local authority has written a statement of provision that the student is entitled to receive from the school. Ask the learning support department if you can see an example of one of these. You may also find that students have Individual Education Plans (IEPs), although these are being phased out and can be replaced by something that is created by individual schools. Once you have all the information you require, you can start to plan your lessons to the students' needs.

For these students, it is about making the learning fun and accessible: use of songs, websites, interactive-whiteboard software, lots of speaking and student interaction.

In our school, we set by ability. In Years 7–9, the lowest of these sets have one 50-minute French lesson a fortnight only. It is important that they get a lot of enjoyment from these lessons, and so the lessons are planned to be full of songs and speaking activities. Students love to use the interactive whiteboard and have fun, all while learning languages.

They are also expected to learn the basic grammar structures and a variety of tenses, but their learning is heavily scaffolded with worksheets and student vocabulary books.

You may find that you have one or more TAs in the classroom with you. It is really important that you know in which lessons they will be with you, as quite often their timetable may change, and they may not be with you every lesson. Ask the learning support department to provide you with a timetable of when there are TAs scheduled to be with you, and which student (if they are supporting a named student) they are supporting.

You will need to guide any teaching assistants that you have with you, so they know what they need to do. Many experienced TAs will be happy to generally support the student, but it is required that you give guidance to them in terms of what you would like them to do for that specific lesson.

The teaching assistant may well not know the language you are teaching, so be prepared to offer them a key-word list for their own use at the beginning of a topic. This will help them to support the students too.

Able students

Learning support also covers the other end of the spectrum, in terms of your most able students.

Differentiating

Students who are identified as able, gifted or talented (AGT) are usually done so as a result of their prior attainment or possibly through cognitive ability tests (CATs). They are those students who have already shown that they have the ability to achieve at a higher level than their peers. On average, they are the top 10 per cent of the cohort.

Able students should be encouraged to learn more than one language, if possible, and also to continue their studies into KS4. It will be these students who are likely to achieve the English Baccalaureate (EBacc), and schools are measured by their percentage of students who achieve this.

The EBacc is awarded to those students who achieve an A*–C grade at GCSE in English, mathematics, science, a language and a humanity subject (either history or geography). As there are guidelines for the KS4 provision of subjects that must be followed, many students will gain the majority of those GCSEs. However, it tends to be a language that many students opt not to continue.

It is a topic that splits opinion, as the percentage of students achieving the EBacc is currently published in the annual school league tables. As a direct result, some head teachers, have chosen to reintroduce languages as a non-optional subject. It could be that some students who are in the ablest category are strongly encouraged to choose a specific 'pathway', which would include a language at GCSE.

Accountability changes that are being introduced by the government from September 2016 will also mean that schools may consider their curriculum provision. This will impact on languages, as this is one of the subjects that will be counted in the eight progress and attainment measures.

Either way, you will undoubtedly have to cater for the ablest in your lessons. Sometimes, the ablest are also the dual linguists and they will learn two languages at KS3. This provides a chance to work together with the teacher of the other language and share strategies or activities that you both do, in different languages, but with the same students.

Currently, I am working with a very able group of Year 7s, teaching them Spanish. I have consulted with their French teacher, and we agree that the majority of them are achieving a high level 3 at the end of their first half-term.

The scheme of work that is currently in place for French doesn't allow for students to have opportunities to move into level-4 work until after the first term. So, after a conversation, we have both decided to develop resources to stretch these students further, so that they can access level 4 before the 'prescribed' time in the scheme of work, which closely follows the textbook they use.

A similar example was when I taught Year 8 the future tense in Spanish a term earlier than planned, so that the students who had achieved their level 4s across the board, and were consistently doing so, could have the opportunity to achieve level 5.

It is all about recognizing the students' needs, their rate of progression, and responding to it. Able students will work at a faster rate; they may not need the amount of consolidation time other students require.

If you are differentiating by outcome, ensure that you include an extension section within the task, so that your abler students have a more challenging opportunity.

These tasks and activities should be shown on the schemes of work and weekly plans, so that, when you are planning, you can use this guidance to ensure that these students are stretched for their own ability.

Provision for the ablest can also be made in the form of enrichment opportunities. This can be through extracurricular clubs, or trips and visits. Local universities may offer curriculum-based days to which students are invited.

Promoting curiosity

One of the things that separate those students who learn a language well from those who perhaps do not is the amount of curiosity that they demonstrate – students who want to know 'why' the language works as it does and the reasons behind the different peculiarities of the different languages. Don't leave interesting explanations for the older students, at GCSE or A level.

There are opportunities for students to discover the reasons why French (or other languages) use different accents, or the origins of certain words. For example, the use of a circumflex usually indicates that a consonant, usually the letter 's', has been removed from the word, for example, *fôret* (forest), *hôpital* (hospital), *hôtel* (hostel), *côte* (coast).

This gives students another way to remember the vocabulary that they are learning. If you need to, do some research into why foreign languages use accents, or the history of the language, and keep some of the information to drop into lessons.

By promoting curiosity within your languages classroom, you may open up different questions from the students, leading to more fascination about languages as a whole. It is really important for students to have the opportunity to understand why a language works as it does, rather than to just accept it for what it is.

Pace and challenge

You will undoubtedly hear the phrase 'pace and challenge' throughout your time training to be a teacher, but what does that mean? In order to address the needs of all of the students in your class, you will need to plan a wide variety of activities and tasks that challenge every student in some way or another. These activities will need to be linked together, with a stepped approach to ensure progression, and there will need to be an element of pace in the lesson. Make sure you give time limits for each task (*vous avez cinq minutes*) and that you keep to it.

Lessons can become boring and stagnant if you, as the teacher, do not link together the tasks, or if they are not planned to develop the learning and, therefore, show progression. You need to always consider the question, 'are all of these students making progress?'.

Allow yourself to stand back sometimes, as the lesson is happening, and consider if the planned activities are working. Are the students engaged? Are the students enjoying the lesson? Are they all on task? Would you enjoy this lesson if you were a student? Is it an interesting lesson? Are the students learning?

If any of the answers to these questions is 'no', then you need to reflect and consider why the answer is no. You may well find it is because there is not enough pace – students are not moving quickly enough – or perhaps the expectations are not high enough. Or, it is because there is not enough challenge – students are finding the work too easy and, therefore, they are not engaged by it.

Either way, pace and challenge are absolutely key in addressing the needs of all of the students in your classroom. You will have to differentiate accordingly to ensure that you achieve the desired level of pace and challenge for all students to learn and make the appropriate amount of progress.

Pattern spotting

Another easy way to stretch some students is to encourage pattern spotting. This could be done when learning new grammar structures, to underline why the language works in a particular way. Pattern spotting can be done by all abilities and can be manipulated into many different types of activity.

Coloured highlighters can be a good tool to use when pattern spotting. Try to keep a collection in your classroom to use.

Tiered entries: foundation versus higher

There is a new curriculum being introduced in 2015, and we know already that the tiers may be removed from GCSE MFL examinations. However, for the time being, students have to enter either foundation or higher tiers. The decision ultimately lies with the classroom teacher, but this can be, and should be, discussed with the students themselves.

With several exam boards, you are allowed to mix and match the tiers. This means that, if a student has a weakness in listening skill, but is a B-grade candidate, you can advise them to consider the foundation-tier paper for the listening test, but continue with the higher tier for the reading paper.

Controlled assessments in speaking and writing are not meant to be tiered and are marked on a scheme that covers all the grades, from A* to G.

You will have time to get the students to practise several past papers, so that you can also gather evidence to back up your professional judgement.

Sharing good, cross-curricular, practice

I remember when I was at my second placement school, I decided to embark on an ambitious project with a Year 10 group; I decided to cover the topic of 'water'. I planned a series of lessons with this group, including vocabulary and new grammar structures that they would learn as part of the overall objective of their group projects.

It was ambitious for me at the time, but, as a student teacher, you have those opportunities to push the boundaries and try new ideas. We covered things from the humanities curriculum, the science curriculum and citizenship. It was a great success, and the students really responded well to it.

Using cross-curricular projects in the languages classroom allows you to develop areas of interest that go beyond the restraints of the curriculum. It also provides opportunities for students of all different abilities to show their strengths.

Ask your mentor if you can observe lessons in the areas where you might like to try cross-curricular work. It is important that you are working together with the other departments, in order not to confuse the students. It is all about using the same terminology, but also about building on what they are doing in that area.

Other suggestions would be to use numeracy to develop surveys, followed by graphs. This can be further developed to use comparative sentences to label a graph. I would approach the maths department to gather information to discuss possible terminology, but also to 'borrow' some graph paper.

You can also develop staff relationships, which can sometimes be difficult, particularly if you are in a large school with 100 or more members of staff. I have also completed a project on different habitats in the world, with the help of the geography department. When it was completed, the geography teacher came and presented me with my own globe and welcomed me as part of his department.

Finally, don't be afraid to display your hard work. The students would be very proud to see their graph work displayed in the classroom, or the corridors. In addition, you could invite those teachers from the other areas to see what you are doing in the languages classroom.

Using language leaders: primary liaison

From September 2014, languages form a statutory subject for all students in KS2 (Years 3–6). This will have a huge impact for the teaching of languages at secondary level. It will mean that students will no longer arrive in Year 7 having no knowledge of a foreign language.

Many secondary schools will have developed, or will be developing, primary links with their feeder schools. You may find that there is someone within the department who goes into the primary schools and works with KS2 children.

As part of your experience as a student teacher, it would be great for you to have the opportunity to go into a primary school and experience for yourself the kind of provision that the KS2 children are receiving.

As a result of this, you could develop some secondary school students as language leaders. This could work for a variety of different ability students, depending on their year group. For example, you could use very able Year 7 or 8 students to develop some exercises to learn vocabulary. They could then go into the primary school and spend some time 'teaching' their tasks to the children.

Another idea would be to take your students in to 'support' the primary school children, so they would take the role of support teachers, maybe one secondary school student to one table.

This kind of thing helps to develop the primary links, but also will hugely support the learning of the language for the secondary school students.

Trips and visits: experiencing the language for real

There is no better way to make the language more relevant than to provide your students with the chance to experience the language in its real context. It is unlikely that you would be expected to organize a trip on your own as a student teacher. However, if there is a possibility to be involved in a trip, or its organization, I would strongly suggest you grasp it with both hands.

When taking the students out of the classroom, you will have an experience that cannot be reproduced in school. Students suddenly develop this urge to want to try the language out for themselves, and those students will experience an immediate sense of satisfaction and gratification.

Do try and watch your students in this situation. I remember very clearly taking students of all ages over to Strasbourg on a trip and going with some of the A level students into the post office. I had taught these students from Year 7. I watched with real pride as they conversed in French with confidence with the tellers and needed no help at all from me to achieve their goal. This was such a great feeling, for the students as well as for me.

Finally, once you have returned from the trip or visit, make sure that you follow it up with some activities in the classroom. You should also make reference to it in the following weeks or terms when teaching.

ACTIVITIES

1   Take one of your classes and create resources for a lesson that will effectively differentiate between certain groups of students. Think about the objective of the lesson and how you can stretch and challenge the abler students, while also supporting those who need it.

2   Approach another department with an idea for a cross-curricular project. Is there a national or local event that you can use as a starting point?

TALKING POINTS

1   How can you differentiate effectively with all of your classes, across the ability range and year groups?
2   What is most important when considering differentiation?
3   What happens if there are native speakers and/or EAL students in your class? How can you support them?
4   Map out a plan for a cross-curricular project. Who could you involve? Where would you look for support, and how could you acquire the necessary resources?
5   Why offer MFL trips? What do students gain from visiting a country where the language is spoken? How can you give those students who cannot go or cannot afford the trip a similar experience to motivate them and their language learning?

6 Using language to explain, question, give feedback

The language that you choose to use, whether in the TL or English, will play a huge role in how the students respond to you, either in the classroom and the corridors, or from feedback in your marking.

When you are observing other teachers, consider the language they are using with the students. It is also really important to reflect upon your own levels of literacy. As a teacher, you are there to facilitate the students' learning, but also to be a role model, and, more than ever, students have to be articulate in all subjects.

Literacy is the responsibility of all teachers and that includes teachers of MFL.

Use of target language

The topic of TL, how much to use it and when to use it, was introduced back in Chapter 1. It remains a slightly controversial topic, and everyone will have their own opinions in terms of when to use it, and when to use English.

When we are thinking about the type of language that we use as teachers to explain, question and give feedback, it is pertinent to consider that what is suggested in this chapter could also be used in the TL.

Students will become used to the language that you choose to use. In one of the departments I worked in, we would distribute

TL sheets to all of our students in French, German and Spanish, which had a list of phrases that might be used in the classroom and also in our marking.

A part of the feedback was to consult this sheet if they did not understand what had been written. Table 6.1 is an example. Students could tick off when they received the feedback and they had understood what it meant.

Positive praise

Praise is so important with all students. Everyone likes to be told that they are doing well and it motivates us all to continue making the effort to succeed. This is particularly true with young people.

Learning a foreign language is difficult for many students, especially as they have to think in a different way to what they are use to. If you continue to give positive praise, you will find that students will respond to that.

Every student will do something well at some stage. It is that moment that you use to build their confidence. A language is the easiest subject for students to give up, to say that they cannot do it, that they don't understand it.

Building on the 'can-do' culture and 'having-a-go' approach, you could praise students for using a grammatical point correctly,

Table 6.1 Example of a target language feedback sheet

French	Tick	English
Bon travail		Good work
Bon effort		Good effort
Attention à la présentation		Careful with presentation
Attention à l'orthographe		Careful with spellings
Très bien fait		Very well done
Tu as oublié les accents		You have forgotten the accents
Il faut apprendre le vocabulaire		You need to learn the vocabulary
Quels beaux dessins		What lovely drawings

even if the pronunciation was incorrect. You could also praise the pronunciation, even if the language that they had chosen was wrong.

Also, the words 'thank you', on the end of phrases or questions, can make a huge difference. It turns something that could be construed as negative into a positive sentence.

Structured feedback

The subject of marking was explored in Chapter 4, but here we are talking about the language that you use when you are marking or giving feedback.

Feedback can be given in the TL, as long as you are sure that the students have a good understanding of it. Usually, I would give some positive comment in the TL, for example, *bravo*, *bien fait*, *bon effort*, and perhaps a sticker or a stamp too.

I would then give the students some idea of the level or grade of the work, although not always, and then some feedback that gives structured information as to how to improve.

Remember, it is important that you use language the students understand, but just as important is what they do with that feedback afterwards.

Targets to improve

Giving targets to improve is the way for students to have clear direction how to make more progress. This is entirely up to you and the language that you choose to use when giving those targets. It may be that the department you are working in has a list of targets that you can use for students to move from a D to a C grade, or an A to an A*. This is a good starting place if you are unsure of the kinds of target to use.

If you don't have any department guidance, it may be an idea to keep a record of the kinds of target you find yourself setting.

Some examples of the targets I set regularly are:

- Make sure that you are learning your vocabulary thoroughly on a regular basis.

- Ensure that you use every opportunity to demonstrate that you can use the future tense as well as a present tense, to show more evidence of working at a level 5.

- Try to use more irregular past participles to show that you understand language higher than a C grade. Learn five irregular verbs and include them in your next written piece.

- Please include three examples of the imperfect tense when describing an event in the past.

- Try to connect your sentences by using more time phrases (*d'abord, après, ensuite, finalement*) or connectives (*parce que, mais, et*).

Questioning

Good questioning is what is required to be able to build on the students' knowledge of the concepts and skills that they are learning. Good questioning not only should address students' ability to remember what they have learned, or what they understand of the language, it also should explore their deeper understanding and thinking to see how much they comprehend of how the language works and why the language works in that way.

Questions can be asked of the whole class, of groups of students or of individuals. The types of question can also be differentiated, depending on the students' ability and the level of language they are achieving.

The most powerful question to ask students is 'why?' In order that you can be reassured that the students understand the many complexities of a foreign language, using the question 'why' will enable you to assess your students' level of knowledge.

Using language to explain, question, feed back

Imagine being in the classroom and teaching a lesson on adjectives to a group of Year 7 students. You think that they understand the basic rules on adjectives, and how they change according to the noun that they are describing.

As a plenary, you could show several sentences with the adjectives highlighted. Some of these sentences would be correct, and some incorrect. Students would have to highlight the wrong ones and change them so they are correct. Once they had done this, you would then ask for feedback.

By not just accepting their answers as right or wrong, and by asking 'why', you would allow the students to really reflect upon the working of the language.

- 'Why is that adjective incorrect?'
- 'Why is that adjective correct?'
- 'Why is the adjective in the wrong position?'
- 'Why does this adjective take an extra "s"?'
- 'Why is this adjective spelled differently, but the meaning is the same?'

When observing other teachers, concentrate on listening to the questions that they ask. Which questions allow the students to really reflect on their learning and make them think? Which questions allow for a rapid response? Do teachers build on questions? Do they accept the first answer and move on? Or do they develop the answer with more questions?

Develop your teaching by the questions that you ask your students. If you are teaching very able students, or A level students, these types of question could well be posed in the TL.

Explaining

In teaching, you will need to vary the type of language you use according to whom you are teaching, which age group and which key stage. The following examples will demonstrate how the register of the language you choose to use to explain language concepts or vocabulary will differ according to different age groups:

- Year 7: beginners' lesson on pets;
- Year 10: grammar lesson on the perfect tense;
- Year 13: A level essay writing.

Year 7

A beginner's lesson on any topic will see you using basic language to ask questions to clarify meanings. In this example, you would start by introducing individual pieces of vocabulary, one at a time:

> le chien, le chat, le lapin, la souris, la tortue, le hamster, le cochon d'Inde

You would make explicit the difference between 'le' and 'la'. You would use choral repetition and some individual or paired student responses. You would use simplified and basic language structures, so that students would learn the foundations of the language to be used, before moving on to add in adjectives, such as the personality or the colour of the pets.

You would ask for examples and expect single phrases in return as a starting point. Depending on the schemes of work, you may be able to refer back to prior learning here and link the learning to adjectives.

I would take the chance to ask the question: 'What is an adjective?' This is to check everyone is in agreement as to what role an adjective plays in the sentence and whereabouts in the sentence you would find it.

Students in Year 7 may still be referring to an adjective as a 'describing word' or even a 'wow word', as used in primary school. There is nothing wrong with this, but the students should now start to be aware of the correct terms for the parts of speech.

Using language to explain, question, feed back

You can build on this learning to add in a connective, such as 'who', allowing the students to expand their responses and give a more complex sentence, showing more developed language skills.

So, when you introduce '*qui*', you might use the term connective, or linking word, or the word that links the two parts of the sentence. You can demonstrate the two parts of the sentence, if they were separated into two sentences. You would probably not use the term subordinate clause or relative pronoun, at this stage.

J'ai un chien blanc qui s'appelle Snowy

The language used in the lesson objective for the beginners' class would be a lot more basic than that for the Year 10 or Year 13 lessons.

Year 10

As your students develop through KS3, they will build their knowledge of the correct grammar terms, not only through MFL lessons, but also through English lessons and their acquisition of literacy expressions from other curriculum areas.

You will see that they are more willing and able to understand and learn the correct terminology when dealing with language.

If you were teaching the perfect tense in French to a group of Year 10 students, you should be able to use terms such as personal pronoun, auxiliary verb and past participle when explaining how to construct this tense. This will support them in becoming more-independent language learners. Remember, you want to develop spontaneity and flexibility within your students: they need to know how the language works to achieve this.

You can be explicit by using colour-coded explanations to split the sentence into three parts, as follows:

1   person or object (personal pronoun/noun);

2   auxiliary verb (*avoir* and *être*);

3   past participle.

You can also now continue to refer to parts of the verb as the infinitive form, or the first/second/third person, singular or plural. Remember too to teach the students the whole paradigm of the verb.

Year 10 students should be starting to accept that these are terms that will be used frequently in their lessons, and you should not shy away from using them. They will get completely fed up with you checking they know what these terms mean, but they will finish their GCSE year with a real knowledge of how to construct language to fulfil their own needs.

Year 13

The A level expectations for MFL are changing and developing as this book is being written. Therefore, the example I will use is based on essay writing.

One of the hardest things for A level students to grasp following the transition from GCSE to A level is the fact that they are required to write much more extensively and more formally. This is usually reflected in the form of an essay.

Years 12 and 13 students are required to be able to write detailed essays full of specific content, but also in excellent TL. You will need to be able to support this through your lessons and through providing opportunities to do this.

Provide your students with some suggested essay starter sentences for them to complete. Give examples, but also allow the students to become independent in their language acquisition.

When I taught A level French, I was very keen to build on students' interest and ability in the French language. TL became much more expected as the form of communication, whether it was spoken or written.

Your use of language for sixth-form students will be more developed, including more language-based terminology and referring to the grammar much more frequently. They will learn from you as you model good language skills.

Using language to explain, question, feed back

Essays will need to be marked for spelling, punctuation, grammar, syntax, as well as content. This may be more challenging for you too.

Therefore, do not shy away from the correct terminology. Invest in a good grammar book and refer to it when you need to. Allow the students to develop their curiosity about the language. If you don't know the answer to a question from an inquisitive sixth-form student, get a second opinion.

As a linguist, you should be able to manipulate and develop the language that you choose to use to explain, pose questions and give feedback. Try deploying a variety of important and useful terminology for all of your students, at all different levels.

ACTIVITIES

1   When you are observing a lesson, make notes about the type of language that the teacher is using when questioning students or giving feedback. Look at the students' books and reflect on the language being used by the teacher in their books.

2   When teaching, decide on a class where you will really think about the type of language that you are using. Is it different depending on the class or the year group?

3   Make a list of targets for feedback to use in students' books as you mark a set of books.

TALKING POINTS

1   Reflect on language and when you speak with the students: when do they respond to you more positively? What language supports the students' learning, and what type of language might hinder them?
2   Compare notes with a colleague on the language that you have observed being used in the classroom.

7 | Ensuring good behaviour

One of the things I was most concerned about when starting out in the classroom was how I was going to ensure that the students behaved in the way that I wanted them to behave.

Your being introduced as a 'student teacher' will not help the behaviour of students. Before you start to teach your classes, agree with your department who you are in front of the students. It may be that they are completely used to having training teachers in their school, and so having you there will not bother them at all.

So, in terms of behaviour, how can you ensure that they meet your expectations?

Making language learning relevant

Students need to understand that what they are learning in their lessons is relevant to them. In order to make languages lessons relevant to your students, you need have some imagination and sometimes be creative in your planning.

Using current affairs and world events that they are aware of will help to engage students in the language.

When I was a student teacher, the World Cup was being held in France. Throughout May and June, matches were played all over France, and many different countries were represented and staying in different towns and cities. It opened up a wealth of opportunities to explore language structures through this medium.

For example, I remember teaching colours to a Year 8 class by showing football strips, and I then developed this further into flags and countries and nationalities. With Year 7, we researched further into the towns and cities where the matches were being held.

I took that one step further and created a large wall display, completely in French, that depicted a huge World Cup matches chart, with all of the countries playing and a map of where they were playing. Once it was created, I asked some of my most challenging Year 9 boys to be responsible for updating the display with the results, the morning following the matches. Their behaviour shifted massively in the classroom, as they became more involved in lessons, participating more willingly and responding more positively to me.

Football may not be everyone's favourite pastime, but it gave me an opportunity to develop materials and to engage students in their learning in a way that was different to other lessons.

These world events that happen regularly, such as the World Cup, the European Championship and the Olympics allow you to develop resources that can be reused, evaluated and improved upon. Don't forget that the Olympic games' official language is French, and during all the coverage you can hear the French language being spoken.

If you engage students in their learning, in whatever way you choose to use, you will see a definite change in their behaviour and their attitude towards you and your lessons.

Cross-curricular opportunities

Chapter 5 also addresses the role of cross-curricular projects and sharing good practice. However, in terms of ensuring good behaviour, this is also a strategy to use to make your lessons interesting to those students who might dislike languages, or for those students in Year 9 (and possibly Year 8) who might not be continuing their language studies at GCSE level.

Using something like a cross-curricular project to spark an interest in languages will need some careful consideration, depending on which group you intend to work with. You could easily do some kind of survey (in the TL) to find out what the students' favourite subjects are. This could be developed further into a numeracy-based activity.

You would need to approach the department with which you are interested in working. The project might be something historical. As an example, I approached the head of history about delivering a short presentation to some of my students on the background of the Occupation of France during the Second World War. This allowed the students to listen to another teacher, whose specialism was pertinent to our learning in French.

It absorbed my students into a world of the past and engaged a lot of the students in something completely different. I was able to build on this interest, and the projects on the role of France in the Second World War were a great success.

Your time as a student teacher is a perfect time to embark on something like this. You have the time to observe other teachers in their subject area before considering a cross-curricular project.

Another way to involve other subjects in the languages classroom is through music and drama. MFL lends itself well to using music and one of the strategies to learn vocabulary and grammar structures is through the medium of song. Students can learn songs in French, or German or Spanish, and hear the correct pronunciation within the songs.

Christmas is a great time to use songs in the classroom and highlight key vocabulary too. It is a good idea to try different things. YouTube has a wealth of foreign songs, and it is very easy to find the lyrics online too.

Using competition

Many children like the idea of being competitive in the classroom. There are regional language competitions that are run by organizations. For example, the 'Have your say' competition is run on an annual basis, and there are regional rounds into which you can enter students. There is also the Languages Spelling Bee.

These competitions are run annually and are for several different languages and for different age groups.

If you enter, or organize, competitions in which students can participate, you may find that students will become more engaged in the language and, as previously stated, they may find it more relevant to them; they will be able to see more clearly why they are learning something.

You could join forces with other subject areas, such as music or drama, to compose a French carol or create a role-play in Spanish for a particular topic. This could then be performed at an expressive arts evening.

Competition does not need to be something that is externally organized. You may want to organize something within your school. As an English assistant in a school near Poitiers, I organized a Valentine's Day card competition. I made a red postbox and placed it in the school library. The students had to create a card and write a poem inside it (in English).

I advertised the competition around the school and in the classes that I worked with, and it became a school-wide competition. I then delivered the cards (with some help) around the school to the other students.

By creating a competition, you are also creating something where students can be more imaginative and use different types of language to help them express themselves. This also promotes and supports more-independent language learning. It can also be a lot of fun for you and for the students.

Praise and rewards

All students like to be praised when they get something right. This includes when students make the choice to behave in the expected fashion. It is really important that students realize that, when they meet the standards that are expected within your classroom, you praise them for it.

Praise and rewards go side by side for me. You will need to find out what the policy is for rewarding students in your school and stick by this. You may find that you can reward through merits or house points or commendations. You can always manipulate this slightly to call them something more pertinent to the language that you are teaching.

However, the same principle remains that, if you praise and reward good behaviour, you will see a positive development in the right direction.

In languages, you may choose to reward students when they participate in lessons by performing a role-play, or when they volunteer an answer. I currently have a small Year 7 Spanish group. When they participate in role-play in Spanish, they receive a miniature Spanish sticker. It doesn't matter whether they got the Spanish correct or incorrect, as I am rewarding their participation. The praise comes alongside that, if they get the language correct.

For beginners, it is important to set out your expectations, and, when those students cooperate with you, you reward them.

Trips and visits

Many students also thrive on the opportunity to go out of school on a trip or a visit. You will find that students will see you in a different light, just as you will see your students differently too. Trips are a great way to develop your teacher–student relationships, and they help to build trust and mutual respect too.

There is no doubt that you will see a difference in the behaviour of students following a successful trip or visit.

Another suggestion is to follow up the trip within a lesson with some form of activity, or, if the students have completed an activity during the course of the visit, then make it valued by spending time feeding back in the lesson.

Students will respond to you in a positive way if they feel that you value their work and their participation in your subject.

Using agreed school terminology

It is a good idea to make sure you know the terminology that the school or department uses. If you want to ensure good behaviour in your classroom, you need to look knowledgeable in terms of your school's or department's procedures.

You may find that your department deals with poor behaviour in a certain way. You may have to give several warnings before you ask for support. You may have to use a system where you write something in the student's planner.

In languages, you will also need to consider whether you use the TL to underline your expectations, or whether you think it is more appropriate to use English. The department may use certain terminology in the TL that you would also need to use, in order to be consistent.

As in many of these situations, do not be afraid to ask what the best course of action is. However, you may need to decide something on your own, on the spur of the moment. Be decisive would be my advice.

If you are consistent in your approach, but also consistent in terms of what your department is doing and what your school is doing, this will support your efforts to ensure that students are behaving appropriately in your class.

Expectations: making the classroom your own environment

One of the great things about being a teacher is that you have your own classroom, your own environment to make yours as you wish it to be. It is the same idea with student behaviour. You set the expectations and you expect the students to adhere to them.

Start off with high expectations. I would strongly advise you not to behave as if you want to be your students' friend. You are the teacher, and they are the students. This is an important relationship and one that is built on mutual trust and respect. However, you have to build this environment; it may well not happen immediately, or without some effort from both parties.

So, set out your stall. How do you want the students to behave? How do you want the students to speak to you? Do you want hands up if they want to ask you a question? Do students have to ask to get out of their seat? Does this have to happen in the TL?

Once you have made a decision on the expectations in your classroom, you must then ensure that you give sanctions to those students who choose not to follow those expectations. You will also need to consult the school's individual behaviour policy.

Your department may well have its own sanctions that are used within the group of languages teachers. This may well support the whole-school behaviour expectations.

Pace and challenge

A section about pace and challenge is also included in Chapter 5, where differentiation is discussed. Pace and challenge are also important considerations when thinking about good behaviour. One of the reasons behind poor behaviour is that students are bored.

In your planning, ensure that there is an ample variety of activities to engage all of the students in your classroom. If the students are misbehaving, then you really should consider whether the students are challenged enough by your teaching.

Look at the plan and think about progression. Are there too many reading or writing activities? If you really need these tasks, can they be done in a different way?

Consider students' learning styles. If you do want to have the written tasks, can they be in a kinaesthetic style rather than a visual style? Try different things and take risks to see what works for you and for your students.

Using realia in the classroom

Once you feel more confident with some of the more challenging students, you could try to introduce some realia into your lessons. Realia is the name for real-life objects that are used in the languages classroom to support learning. They support a more active teaching and learning environment, where students can touch, see and hear real objects.

As suggested later, in Chapter 12, if you go to the country of the language you teach, you could collect some realia while you are there. These could include:

- city maps;
- train/bus timetables;
- train/bus tickets;
- CDs of songs in the TL;
- French/German/Spanish versions of Monopoly/Scrabble/Guess Who;
- restaurant menus;
- newspaper articles;
- photographs;
- supermarket flyers showing food and drink promotions.

In terms of how to use them, documents such as timetables, tickets, restaurant menus and city maps could be used when explaining how systems work in the country. They could also be used to support role-play situations, to try and make them more real.

CDs of songs are a great resource. You can search for the lyrics online and then use them for exercises for students to listen to and complete gaps where you have removed a word.

Family-favourite board games also exist in France, Germany, Spain, Italy etc. They have their own versions. These are great fun to play in the classroom, particularly as an end-of-term treat. Although they are super to play with A level students, try to organize groups so you can play them with the younger students too. You may be surprised to see that, in Scrabble, the letters are worth different values. In French, the letter Z, for example, is only worth 1 point.

Photographs are also a very interesting resource for students, particularly if they have never been to the country. For example, do your students know that, in France, the postboxes are yellow? Take pictures of things that are different, but also take pictures of road signs, or signs on shop windows. All these can be used in the classroom to help bring the language to life.

Other suggestions would include magnetic words that you can buy in bookshops. I have seen these magnetic words in French and German, and I have also seen them work in the classroom very effectively to support creative writing or poetry.

Try to make sure you have some dice to hand, as you can use them for speaking tasks.

Finally, stuffed toys can make a lesson on prepositions more exciting, as you can use them to demonstrate positions. You could also use them for dialogue too.

ACTIVITIES

1   Collect as much realia as you can to use in your classroom – see suggestions above.

2   Use praise and rewards in your classroom. Invest in some stickers to support the praise.

3   Create some resources to use that are based around the students' interests.

TALKING POINTS

1   Think about a class that is challenging you in terms of behaviour. Why do you think this might be? Can you observe the class in another subject? Do the students behave differently with a different teacher? Why could this be?

2   Consider what your expectations are in your classroom. What behaviour will you prioritize as being absolutely unacceptable? What can you do to ensure that students are adhering to these expectations?

8 Dealing with observations

Throughout your teaching career, there will be a lot of observations. Some teachers find it very difficult to have other people in their classrooms; others are more at ease.

As a student teacher, and then a newly qualified teacher (NQT), there will be many observations to track your learning as a developing teacher, as well as to check that you are meeting teacher standards.

You should be given some warning of an official observation of this kind, so that you can plan accordingly. You may have targets that you are working on with your mentor, and these will need to be demonstrated in the lesson.

Planning

Once you know when someone is coming to observe you, you can start to think about the lesson. You will need to consider the lessons beforehand too, and what is on the scheme of work for these students at this time.

For an observation lesson, the easiest type of lesson to show progress is either a 'lead' lesson, where you are introducing a new topic for the first time, or a grammar lesson.

If you want to deliver either type of lesson, you will need to do some preparation in the lessons that precede this lesson. For example, if you are going to teach the first 'lead' lesson on healthy living, the students may well need prior knowledge (or revision) on food and drink vocabulary.

If you choose to plan a lesson on the perfect tense in French, the students may need prior knowledge on, or reminding about, the auxiliary verbs *avoir* and *être*.

You want the observation lesson to show off your very best work, and this includes excellent planning skills. You will become more at ease with other people observing your lessons in time.

In every lesson, it is important to motivate your students to learn, but especially so in an observed lesson. Think about the kinds of task that you already know work and will motivate your students.

Avoid doing structured vocabulary tests during an observation. Although they are a useful way to check prior learning and a comfortable structure for many students, they can take too much time out of a lesson that is being observed.

Consider the tasks that you are planning. They need to be linked in some way and stepped, so that you are using the previous task and learning to support the following tasks.

For example, if you are teaching a lesson on directions, make sure that you revise vocabulary for places in the town first. Once the students have been refreshed on places in the town, you can remind them of the importance of remembering the gender of the vocabulary. You will need this later on, when you come to teaching prepositions to describe position.

Perhaps plan a vocabulary-matching activity, where you have listed the vocabulary and want the students to match it to the English (see Table 8.1).

Using something like this, the students can recap their vocabulary, see clearly the genders of the nouns and match them up to the English. They can use this for the remainder of the lesson to check their vocabulary if they forget something.

Dealing with observations

Table 8.1 Example of a vocabulary-matching sheet

En ville	In the town
Un cinéma	Market
Un magasin	Stadium
Un château	Supermarket
Un stade	Swimming pool
Un restaurant	Square
Un café	Cinema
Un marché	Train station
Un supermarché	Restaurant
Un musée	Bus station
Une piscine	Castle
Une gare	Chemist
Une gare routière	Church
Une pharmacie	Museum
Une place	Shop
Une église	Café

At the same time as highlighting the genders, remind the students of the use of *à* and how it changes when a masculine, feminine or plural noun follows.

> *Pour aller au cinéma s'il vous plaît?*

> *Pour aller à la pharmacie s'il vous plaît?*

The following step would be to teach prepositions such as 'next to', 'opposite', 'in between', 'to the right of', 'to the left of', etc. Once again, by highlighting the genders, this will link to teaching the students how *de* changes, depending again on the succeeding noun.

> *Le cinéma est à côté du stade.*

> *La pharmacie est en face de l'église.*

In a sequence of tasks, you are then building on the students' learning for them to be able to achieve the overall lesson objective of, in this example, giving and understanding directions, using prepositions.

The planning must clearly show that the students are making progress throughout the lesson, in order to achieve the lesson objective.

Evidence of progress

One of most important things observers will look for in your lesson will be evidence of progress: what do the students know at the end of the lesson that they did not know at the beginning? How much learning has taken place? How much progress have all of the students made?

As already suggested, one of the ways to do this is through a grammar lesson or a lead lesson on a new topic area. Of course, this is not always possible. So, how can you demonstrate to the observer that your students are making sustained progress?

Observers will look at books and consider progress over time, not only progress that has happened in your lesson. Observers will also talk to the students and probably look at student planners to check for regularity of homework.

Progress and assessment do go hand in hand, and so Chapter 4 will also help when thinking about ways to track progress.

It may feel unnatural to be so overt, but it is necessary to be explicit when showing that the students are making progress in your classroom. This can be done in several ways.

Students should be able to work independently, to build on the language objectives for the lesson. Something like a tick list to check learning or traffic light progress checks are simple, but effective, ways to check learning throughout the lesson.

You do not need to stop the lesson completely to check progress. You can move around the room, evaluating the students' learning and supporting where necessary.

Using the language for real purposes, where students have to find information to fill a gap, is another way to check their progress.

Dealing with observations

Student progress must be evidenced, but every student in your classroom should be making progress, regardless of his or her ability. You have to be sensitive to the needs of all of your students. It may be an idea for your observer to have an overview of any data tracking you may have already done with your class over the course of the half-term or topic area. In this way, your observer will be able to be clear as to who is starting at which level.

Target language

One trap not to allow yourself to fall into during an observation is to do something that your students are not used to. A fine example of this is your use of TL. If you use TL regularly, and for specific things such as greetings or instructions, then it is appropriate to continue to do so.

Do not attempt to conduct the whole lesson in TL in an effort to impress your observer. The students will be completely confused, and this could lead to a potentially difficult situation.

You know how much TL is appropriate to your students and to each individual class. Remain focused on this and do not be tempted to try something new.

As long as you know your students, you can take control in terms of student TL during an observation. Make sure you ask, not only those students who you know will deliver a good level of language, but also those students who you know will answer and not freeze up when put on the spot. Consider differentiation too and approach the abler students first, and then move towards the less able, once they have heard a good example.

Consider pairings when using speaking tasks. I have often moved students around so that the abler can support the less able or more timid students. I have also paired students by ability, allowing the abler to be challenged by the language, and allowing me or the TAs to support the less able in their speaking.

The key thing is to behave in the way your students are used to. Relax and use your TL, and they will too.

Be clear about what amount of TL is expected from the students during the lesson. Students respond well to clarity, as well as consistency.

If you are using PowerPoint slides or self-made worksheets, double and triple check your language. It is never good to have a spelling mistake or an accent in the wrong place, but in particular it is not during an observation lesson, if another languages specialist is observing you; this may bring into question your subject knowledge.

Flexibility

The more you teach, the more comfortable you will become at being flexible with your lesson plan. You will need to be able to respond to the rate at which your students react to your teaching.

If, for example, you are teaching a Year 10 class and you are introducing the topic of education and work, and the students cannot remember the school subject vocabulary from their Year 7 or 8 work, then you will need to do some revision on that vocabulary before moving on to other language structures.

Do not presume that your students know something that you haven't taught to them. Another example is teaching the students the time in the TL. Many students may not know how to read a clock face, and so this may need to be completed first.

It is important that you become at ease with your lesson plan and are able to be flexible according to the needs of your students and unpredictable elements of a lesson.

Reliability of students

This moves smoothly into the topic of how reliable your students will be for you when there is someone else in the room. You may well find that the observations are completed with a class of your choice, or it may be dictated by when the observer is available to come and see your lesson.

Dealing with observations

You may find it easier to tell your students that someone is coming in to have a look at the lesson and see what you are all achieving within the class.

Most of the time, students will rise to the occasion, producing good language when they are in the spotlight. If you have prepared those students appropriately, and do not surprise them with anything they are not used to, the students should respond well.

If you use the kinds of task that the students are used to doing, whether they be listening or speaking tasks, and they are confident in performing these tasks, then there should be no reason for the students to respond negatively.

If you do experience poor behaviour during a formally observed lesson, then follow the school policy on behaviour management. Make sure that you go through the correct procedure, and, if you need to ask for further support through an 'on-call' system, then don't be afraid to do so. Be careful not to ignore poor behaviour.

Enjoyment and interest

Your observations should take place once you have had a chance to settle into your classes and embed your personal expectations. Once the students are fully aware of the way that you teach and how you want them to behave in your classroom, the enjoyment and interest will undoubtedly develop naturally.

Students who are engaged in the lesson content and who are happy and at ease in your classroom environment will enjoy their lessons with you.

This will also be reflected when your lessons are observed. You cannot set up students to look interested or feign enjoyment; this comes with time. By being consistent in your approach, you will see how the students will respond positively to that.

Use of iRIS

If you are unaware of iRIS, it is a company that has created a camera that can be placed in classrooms for observation purposes. You can search on the Internet for the spiel, but it is a tool that can be used to develop all teachers in the classroom.

It may be worth asking someone at your school if they have an iRIS camera in school, and how you set about booking it for your own class.

You can learn an awful lot by watching yourself teach. Once you have got over the embarrassment of cringing at yourself and your mannerisms, you can really learn a lot by reflecting on your own practice.

No one has to see it, apart from you, if you do not want to share it. At the other end of the spectrum, your mentor could be observing you from the next-door classroom or from their office, on the real-time recording. There is also a feature where your mentor could talk to you through a headphone that you wear.

You have to wear a microphone, which is worn around the neck, so that the sound of you and your students can be picked up. This could be a great way to check your own language, or measure the amount of TL that is used in the class.

To be able to record and keep these lessons for your own use, as well as to be able to share, is an invaluable resource for developing teachers. If you can have a go, I would strongly suggest that you go for it.

ACTIVITIES

1   Video yourself teaching a class. Look at your micro-mannerisms. Where do you stand? What do you do with your hands? Do you use 'OK' too much? Reflect on your own teaching once you have recorded yourself and think

about how you could make small changes to have the biggest impact.

2   Ask another student teacher to observe you and gather their opinion too.

3   Create some student questionnaires and find out what their opinions are in terms of your lessons. Be careful to think about the questions carefully first.

4   Before any observation, ensure that you are made aware of when it is and what they are coming to observe. Is there a specific area that they will concentrate on, such as questioning, for example?

5   Look at your lesson plan for the observation. What you want the students to achieve? How can you make the progress explicit?

TALKING POINTS

1   How do you feel when you are being observed? Does it change depending on the group or not?
2   Do you think your teaching changes when you are being observed?
3   How can you make observations an integral part of being a teacher?
4   How can you demonstrate progress over time within an observed lesson? What evidence will you need?

9 Dealing with pressure

An inevitable part of teaching and becoming a teacher, as in many professions and walks of life, is pressure. What is important is how you deal with the stress that comes with the pressure points of teaching life.

Many teachers will say that the autumn term is the hardest term. Unfortunately, this is also your first term as a teacher. The autumn term tends to be the longest term, and it is the time when the days get shorter, and it gets light later in the morning and dark earlier in the evening. Don't underestimate what impact that will have on your working life.

There are small differences that you can make in order to make things easier for you and for those around you.

Communication

It is vital to communicate well with your mentor, your tutor, your head of department or faculty. If you think that the pressure is getting worse, you must talk to someone. This may be a colleague, another student teacher or someone in authority.

You might find that you have settled well into your classes, and the teaching is going well, but then something you might not have expected happens.

Dealing with pressure

Email is an easy and quick way to communicate at any time of the day. However, you may have to wait for an answer. Also, remember that an email isn't as effective as talking to someone, in the majority of cases.

If you find yourself dealing with a personal issue, such as a death in the family, you need to share this information, as it may well impact on you in the classroom.

If you choose not to communicate your concerns, pressure may well build until such a time that you will be less able to cope with the day-to-day interactions with other colleagues, as well as the students.

Colleagues

Your fellow teachers are the most valuable resource that you will have as a teacher. Remember, all teachers have been student teachers. They will all have their own anecdotes and memories to tell you that may well be funny, uncomfortable or inspirational for you when you are at a low ebb.

We all started somewhere. We have all experienced the first time in a classroom in front of a class of eager students wanting to learn, or those students who are the opposite, sitting staring at you in anticipation.

I remember losing my cool in a Year 9 French class in one lesson during my teacher placement and swearing by mistake. I was devastated. I knew I had shown a weakness, but I also was terribly worried about parent complaints.

I immediately went to see my head of department, who was reassuring in a way that said, 'it happens to us all' and 'don't worry'.

Many things can be resolved by sharing your worries and concerns with those around you, especially other student teachers who are in the same position as you. By sharing your woes with other teachers, you will certainly be reassured that you are not alone, that things can be rectified and you will get the support you need.

If your colleagues are unable to support you or give you the advice that you need, they should be able to point you in the right direction.

Open-door classroom

My first job was in a relatively tough school in Harlow, Essex. The experience set me up for my career, but it was very stressful and quite difficult at times. What I noticed at the time, and continue to reflect on, were the support and the camaraderie of the whole staff.

The majority of the teachers taught their lessons with their doors open. There was this unwritten agreement that, if you were struggling with a group or an individual, another teacher would support you. It was a mutual 'open-door policy'.

I still find myself teaching with my door open. I want my classroom to feel as though anyone is welcome, but also that I am not hiding away and isolating myself from the rest of the school.

Understandably, this may not always be possible. Teaching languages is often a noisy process, especially when students are all talking to one another in the language that they are learning. You do have to be sensitive to those classrooms around you and the tasks that the students are doing in those classrooms.

It may be that you don't feel comfortable opening your door, especially if you are dealing with difficult behaviour. All you can do is to try it out and see if it works for you.

Time for reflection

Throughout your time training to be a teacher, you will be encouraged to reflect on all of your lessons: what went well, and what could be improved. This reflection time is vital to your development as a teacher and to your considering your own approach to teaching.

Dealing with pressure

This type of reflection is almost enforced as a student, and you may find yourself becoming a bit fed up with it, especially as you become more adept at teaching.

However, finding time for reflection, especially at times of high levels of stress or pressure, is more difficult. Try just taking a step back and look at your areas of pressure or stress from a different perspective.

You could try investing in a relaxation CD to force you to stop and relax for 20 minutes. However silly it sounds, it works. You need to try all kinds of different things to relax and enable yourself to reflect on what is a highly pressurized environment at times.

Planning forward

All schools have a school calendar that shows all of the school events across the course of the year. If you are not given a calendar like this, then ensure that you ask for a copy.

You can use this calendar to plan forward your half-terms, terms and the whole year. You will see that there may be pressure points across the year, especially at parents' evenings or report writing for your classes. You may not be wholly responsible for those at this stage, but I would imagine that you would be expected to have an input.

As the year progresses, think about when those pressure points appear. Reflect back on them and then consider how, when you are teaching full time in the following year, you can plan forward to ease some of that pressure.

Does being involved in school trips become a stressful experience? Ask yourself why? When thinking about organizing your own trips or visits in the future, how can you plan forward to avoid as much of this pressure as possible.

One of the good things in teaching is that it is cyclical. Once you have been teaching or been in a school for a year, you can consider what went well, and, when that event or period of time comes around again, how you can make things easier for yourself next time.

Work–life balance

Your choice to become a teacher is one that will affect, not only you, but also those people around you, especially outside school. During your student teacher days, and possibly more so in your first year, you will talk about nothing but school and your students.

Everyone has had an experience of being at school as a student, and so, at times, this makes people think that they know what it must be like to be a teacher. Many people will have advice to share with you, some good and some not so good.

At times, this may not help you in striking the right work–life balance.

There will be times when you will be working very long hours, some weeks more than others. As a student, I would always stop work by 10 p.m. I would never work past 10 p.m., and I still stick to that.

If you are working ridiculously long hours, planning, marking or making resources, you will not be on your best form for teaching the following day.

Working very long hours is not sustainable. You may have the school holidays, but, when working very long hours, the weekends are not long enough to recover, and you will probably be working at least one of the weekend days.

I work on either Saturday or Sunday, but never both. I have a life, and a family, and want to be able to enjoy that time too.

Your work–life balance may well be moulded according to your mentor, or head of department, and their expectations. For example, my current head teacher shuts our school at 6 p.m. She does not want anyone on the premises after this, and so we have to go home at 6 p.m. The school is open from 7 a.m., and so she considers this enough time for staff to be able to be on site.

In addition, it is very easy to work long hours and communicate with others through email. Check the times that you are sending emails. What does it say if you are emailing people at midnight, or at 4 a.m.?

Dealing with pressure

As a student teacher, or a new teacher, you should be able to balance your work and life accordingly. If you are finding yourself spending an immense amount of time planning, then ask for help – ask someone how to plan more effectively, or ask someone to look at your planning with you.

This takes us back to the beginning of the chapter: when things are getting stressful, talk to someone about it.

Diet and exercise

Sitting alongside the importance of achieving the correct work–life balance is the importance of a good diet and doing some form of exercise.

Many teachers fall into a very easy trap of not eating properly at school, because they do not have the time, or they have clubs at lunchtime or duty during breaktime. It is vital that you eat something during the day. Get yourself into the habit of having good, healthy snacks in your bag that you can dig into when you are getting tired, or when you only have time to grab something quickly.

If you don't eat properly, your energy levels will drop, and you may find yourself more susceptible to becoming ill and then need time off school.

In addition to this, but at times not as easy, try to ensure that you eat a good meal in the evening, at home. If you find that you don't have the time or the inclination to cook at home, then eat a good lunch at school.

Exercise is also something that will help with stress levels and keeping you fit and healthy. Making the effort to get out and do something, even if it is just a walk around the town, or nearby, will help to raise your levels of endorphins and have a positive impact on your health.

For me, exercise is the first thing that has to be moved or not completed as the work pressure mounts. In fact, this is probably counter-productive, as it is even more important during these stressful times, to help deal with the pressure.

Sleep

It is true that people are different in terms of how much sleep they need, but everyone needs sleep to be able to function properly. Try not to burn that candle at both ends, and make yourself go to bed at a reasonable time on school nights.

Teaching is not a job where you can hide away when you feel under the weather, or when you have not had enough sleep. You are always on show and 'performing' in the classroom. Your students expect you there to facilitate their learning, and this is your job. Getting enough sleep is another vital part of this, for you to be able to deal with each day.

Relationships

You may need to remember to nurture relationships outside school as well as in school. Friends who are not teachers or student teachers may not be able to empathize with your stresses or your issues of the moment. Many will listen, I am sure, but many may become less tolerant of hearing about your pressures and strains at school.

Remember, these people know you and love you for who you are, and you may change during times of pressure.

My husband likes to highlight to me when, during the holidays, I return to my normal self.

When you are working long hours, and when you decide to turn down an offer of a social occasion, or the dinner is late, remember your work–life balance. It is so important to spend time with those people who might not be in teaching, but who enjoy being with you too. Don't forget those people in the melee of training to be a teacher.

School holidays and weekends

Teachers currently work 39 weeks of the year and have 13 weeks holiday. Some people will say that teachers work 'part-time'. You will find out soon enough that the majority of teachers will work at some point during their holidays. You only need to scan Twitter to see how many educationalists are writing blogs or linking to educational articles, either through the weekends or over the holidays.

If you are able to, I would strongly suggest getting some time away in the first half-term holiday. My family and I make a point of getting to the coast in October, and we usually all get into the sea too, with wetsuits! It is invigorating, yet relaxing. We walk on the beach, in the wind and the rain. It is cold, yet I love every minute and, most importantly, I relax.

This sets me up for the second part of the autumn term and the run up to Christmas.

School holidays and weekends are the time when you recover, relax and then prepare for the next part of your teaching week or term. This is why it is important to use the time wisely. Plan your holidays too, so you have something to look forward to when things do get pressurized at school.

You may be a parent, which is great for school holidays. However, your holiday becomes the time you look after your child(ren). Try, if you can, to have some time for yourself, not preparing or working for school. This is also really important.

TALKING POINTS

1   Discuss your plans for your first holiday. Exchange ideas on how you will find time for some relaxation.
2   Reflect on how you can ensure that you have a decent work–life balance. Where is your tipping point?
3   Talk to your friends and family outside the school environment and ask them to highlight to you when you are demonstrating signs of pressure or stress.
4   Talk to your colleagues about how they ensure a work–life balance.

10 Applying for your first post

Finding a vacancy

During your training year, the time will come when you want to apply for a job. Job adverts will start to appear in the spring term of your training year for the following September start. It is a good idea to make yourself aware of where these adverts might be found.

The *Times Educational Supplement* website is a good place to start. Local papers and school websites are also a place to keep your eye on for vacant positions.

You may have an idea of where you would like to teach; you may know a school or a town where you would prefer to be.

There are a wide variety of schools, and each will have a different emphasis to its philosophy of education. You may or may not prefer to work at a faith school. You may feel that you would like to work in an academy or a free school. You may be looking at a private school or specifically a state school. You may not have any preference for the time being.

You will be starting to build up your own views on education throughout your training year, and these may hold an importance for you when you are looking for a position for your first year in teaching.

You should consider the kind of school you want to apply to, the languages that are taught and what you can offer to the school too.

Specialist schools are no longer funded by the government, but many schools have chosen to continue to offer more opportunities in a certain curriculum area, because the specialism has been well received and has been successful. There may well be a 'languages' school in your area at which you would be keen to work.

In my local area, there are a couple of schools that offer the International Baccalaureate in the sixth form, instead of A levels, following GCSE study. This may be something that interests you too.

There are some schools that advertise for their languages teachers in the TL and expect the application to be written in the language too.

If you are a dual linguist, you need to consider if you want to be able to teach both languages.

Schools will be restricted as to languages that they can offer by the teaching staff that they have, and the languages that those teacher offer. You may be able to offer something new.

Once you find a vacancy, you will need to consider whether this is a school you would like to work in, what languages it offers, whether you know anyone who has trained or currently works in the school, and whether you want to apply for the position. Is it right for you?

In order to help you make that decision, there is usually an information pack that you can request, either by email or telephone. You will need this information pack to make your application relevant and pertinent to the position that is available. You might find the information on the school website.

Writing a letter of application

When you start to think about applying for a job, it might be a good idea to start considering what you would include in your letter of application. Start by thinking about who you are and what your own educational philosophy is.

Applying for your first post

This letter is very similar to a personal statement. It is this letter that will introduce you to your potential future employer. It needs to achieve the right balance of who you are, what you have achieved so far, what you would like to achieve and, most importantly, why you want to have the chance to work at that school.

This is the letter that will lead to an interview. It is important that it reflects you and who you are.

Before you send your letter anywhere, it is a good idea to ask someone to read it for you. Ask someone who has written letters of application before, or someone who has received letters from people applying for jobs. Don't be shy about asking someone to read it; they may well have some very good advice.

Once you have received the information pack, you will see that it may well include a person specification for the position available. Go through this meticulously and highlight those requirements that you have and those that you may be working towards.

When writing your letter, refer to the person specification and to your skills and attributes.

You will need at least a paragraph that refers specifically to your subject knowledge, whether it is French, German, Italian, Spanish, etc. Explain why you decided that you wanted to become a languages teacher.

Within this paragraph, it is important to outline some examples of your experience of your own language learning, either from your school days or higher education. You will also need to explain some of your own teaching experience here too.

Draw on specific examples. Explain a lesson that has gone particularly well and describe why you think it was so successful. You could also explore something that you have done that meant you collaborated with another teacher, or a cross-curricular project.

However, try not to give all of the information; you want to leave room for your interviewers to want to know more detail about these examples.

Potential employers want to see what you have achieved already, but also would like to see what your own potential is. If you have been included on any school trips or visits, or involved in extra-curricular clubs, include this information too.

This is likely to be your first job and, therefore, your NQT year. It is vital that you feel that this is the right position in the right school for you.

You should research the school fully and, in your letter, give reasons why you are interested in working at that particular school. It is likely that you will be asked this at interview, so you will need to consider this anyway.

Once the letter is completed, make sure that it is no more than two pages long and read it through to check spelling and grammar. Your potential employer will place a lot of importance on your level of literacy, and this will be the first formal written piece that he or she will read from you. Take the time to ensure that it is accurate. As suggested previously, ask someone to read it through for you.

Before sending it off, make sure that it is addressed to the right person, as requested in the information pack. The school may prefer hard copies rather than email, this is another thing worth checking, if it is not specified in the information pack.

Completing the application form

It is very likely that you will have to complete an application form of some kind. If the school that you are applying to is a local authority school (and not an academy), the form is likely to be a standard local authority application form. Some schools may have their own application form that they require you to complete. A few schools may require you to send a curriculum vitae.

What is important is that you do what is required by the specific school to which you are applying. If you do not follow its specifications, it is unlikely that you will be called for interview.

Take your time to complete the application form. You may well end up completing several of these. Check if you can complete it on your computer, or whether it should be handwritten. Read carefully what the application form requires you to include.

Applying for your first post

I have received application forms with spelling mistakes on the front page. If you have many forms to read through, and there are mistakes from the beginning, it is likely that the form with mistakes will be discarded. Don't forget to check this too.

The form, alongside your letter, will be the information that is needed to win you the opportunity to be invited for interview.

The right school for you

Getting the right job is a vital component of experiencing a successful NQT year. However, you may find that vacancies do not appear in the school(s) that you are looking at, or that you are interested in.

You have to start somewhere, and that is looking for a vacant position. You may be fortunate that a position becomes available in your training school, so that you can really consider, with first-hand experience, whether you would like to work there on a permanent basis. There will be advantages and disadvantages to this.

Some questions to consider when looking for a job:

- Is the position for a teacher of one or more languages in which I specialize?
- Is the position full time or part time?
- Is this a position for an NQT?
- Is this a permanent position?
- Where is the school?
- How far is the commute?
- Which languages are taught?
- What extracurricular clubs are offered?
- What could I offer?
- How big is the school?

- Does it have a sixth form?
- Is A level teaching important to me at this point?
- Is there a website?
- How much information can I glean from the website?
- Do the school have a Twitter feed or Facebook page?
- Is it featured in the local media?
- What is the school's vision?
- Does its vision coincide with my own?
- Has it got a recent Ofsted report?
- Where is the school at in terms of Ofsted rating?
- Is this important to me?
- Can I go and visit the school before applying?

These questions are a good starting point for you to organize your thoughts when seeing a vacant position in which you might be interested.

It is always a good idea to enquire to see if you can go and have a look around the school, before the closing date for applications. That is really the only way to get a better idea about the school itself, and whether you feel you would fit in to the school or not. Make sure you visit the languages department.

I remember visiting a school as a student teacher looking for my first position. We toured the school, and the person giving the tour left the languages department until the end. The department was placed at the end of a dark corridor and was, quite frankly, bleak.

The school was a very good school and had a great reputation. I was keen to work there until I visited. I left the school with a real sense of disappointment. In my opinion, the school, and the person conducting the tour, did not consider the languages department important to the success of the school. I didn't apply there.

The school should 'feel' right. I remember someone saying that to me and I was a little cynical and didn't really believe them.

Applying for your first post

That was until I set foot in the school where I was successful in getting my first teaching post. The deputy head teacher showed me round the school and I immediately loved it. I am sure that this genuine enthusiasm comes across. I felt it was the right school for me and said so at my interview.

Do remember, it is likely that the person showing you around will feed back to the head teacher, so you should act as though you are at an interview. You should dress and speak accordingly.

The big sell

If you are called for interview, there may not be much time between the closing date and the interview date. So, you need to prepare yourself for each job throughout the application process, making you ready for interview if you only get a short period of notice for this.

During the time you are applying for a job, it might be an idea to consider what you are going to say if you do get an interview. Remember that the people who interview you are very likely to have your application form in front of them.

Make sure you keep a copy of the letter. You want to develop your experiences that you have outlined in your letter at interview, so make sure you are ready for that too.

I would find some really quiet and concentrated time to think about yourself. What kind of teacher do you want to be? Can you reflect on some of the teachers you have observed and pick out the best parts, or even the worst parts? Teaching is a very personalized profession; it is what you make it to be. As a new teacher, you have the world open to you, and you can develop in any which way you would like to. Making sure that you get the right environment to be able to do that is paramount.

Once you have considered your own skills, attributes and educational philosophy, compare that with all of the information you have about the school. Do you think they are compatible? Once you have visited the school, consider your experience here too. If it all fits together, then go for it.

Prepare yourself fully for the big sell.

ACTIVITIES

1   During your training year, keep a log of activities that you are involved in around the school, such as cross-curricular projects, extracurricular clubs, trips and visits and what impact you think they had on you, your teaching and the students.

2   Reflect on your own teaching experience as you go along. Keep a reflection log when you have a great lesson and think about why it was so good. Reflect on the more challenging lessons too, if you changed your approach, and if this had any impact.

3   Consider any interests out of school. If you write these things on your application, you may need to be able to follow this up at interview.

4   Practise writing an application letter, so that you can tweak it to suit the job and the school to which you apply.

TALKING POINTS

1   Discuss jobs that might interest you with your colleagues. Should you apply? Ask for their opinion.

2   Discuss the application process with another student teacher when applying for a position. Have you come across the same hurdles? Can you support one another?

11 Interview advice and likely questions

Starting again

Your application form and letter enable you to introduce yourself to a certain extent. These two things, and perhaps a pre-application visit, will get you an interview.

You will need to start over once you arrive for interview. Do not take for granted that the people who are interviewing you will remember everything you have written in your application.

You may have a very strong application letter and pertinent experience for the job, but then you have to sell yourself on the day and show yourself to be the best person for the job.

Interview lesson

It is highly likely that you will have to teach during your interview day. That is not unusual, and you should be prepared to do this. The school want to see you teach – that is what they will be employing you to do – and so you will need to perform on the day.

Information should be made available to you as soon as you receive your invitation to go for an interview. You may be given a specific topic and time limit.

Examples of an interview lesson:

- You will be required to teach a 50-minute lesson on the topic of 'Illness' to a group of twenty, top set, Year 8 students. This will be their first lesson on this topic.
- You will be required to teach a 20-minute lesson introducing superlatives to a group of mixed Year 9 students. They have only been learning Spanish since the beginning of Year 8.
- You will be required to teach a 60-minute lesson to a group of Year 10, set 3 students, to develop their knowledge of using two different tenses together.

It is possible that you will not have any further information. You may even have less information. I know someone who was asked to come and teach their 'best lesson'. Usually, the school will give you a contact name and email address so that you can ask any further questions.

Possible questions to gain more information might be:

- How many students are in the class?
- Is there an interactive whiteboard in the room?
- Can I have a list of student names?
- At what levels are the students achieving?
- Are they dual linguists? (It might be possible to link languages to support the learners.)
- Are they using a specific course book? (Try to ascertain what they might already know at this stage.)
- Are there computers available for the students to use?
- Do I need to bring a laptop?
- Will I get some time before the lesson to set myself up?

Planning the interview lesson

Once you know what the guidelines or expectations are for your lesson, you should approach it like you would any other observed lesson. Try to think carefully about objectives and timings. You should consider student progress too. These three things must be made explicitly clear throughout the lesson.

- What are the objectives? What do you want the students to achieve during the lesson?

- How long have you got? How many tasks do you want to include in the lesson? Are they teacher-led or student-led? Can you add a variety of activities to demonstrate different skills?

- How will you demonstrate student progress?

Once you have decided on the objectives, timings and tasks, you will need to create or manipulate some resources. Again, consider the learning styles of the students. Are you going to use an interactive whiteboard? Are you going to use PowerPoint slides? What about your kinaesthetic learners?

Target language

So, you have got your interview date and the requirements of the lesson, and you have planned your lesson. The next question to ask yourself is how much TL should you use.

As already discussed at length back in Chapter 1, TL can be a controversial topic for languages teachers.

- How much TL is appropriate?
- What will the students be used to?
- How good will they be at the language?
- Will they understand me?
- What if they don't understand me?

The bottom line is that you have to use some TL. You are being observed to see if you can meet the job requirements, and, as a foreign language teacher, you will need to demonstrate your subject knowledge.

One thing I always do if I am asked to teach in an interview situation is to find a way to learn the students' names. This can be done quickly in a variety of ways. You can use sticky labels and distribute them once the students have answered a question in the TL. This way, you are able to ascertain their level of language too.

Comment t'appelles-tu?

Je m'appelle Abby.

Merci. Voici ton sticker. Ecris ton nom dessus s'il te plaît.

Another suggestion would be to ask a variety of simple questions, asking their names and noting them down on a rough table plan (created once you were allowed to get into the classroom to set yourself up).

The final suggestion is to have table nameplates ready on their desk and ask them to write their names on them as soon as they sit down. Again, this instruction could be done in the TL, while you demonstrate writing your name on your table nameplate.

Bonjour tout le monde. Il y a une feuille de papier sur votre table [hold up paper]. *Ecrivez votre nom ici et mettez-la sur la table. Merci.*

Within the first 5 minutes, you can easily find out who are the strongest and weakest students in the room. Once you have their names, you can ask the students directly to answer a question, rather than depending on them to put their hands up.

Some questions might include (in the TL):

* What is your name?
* How old are you?
* Where do you live?

Interview advice and likely questions

- Do you have any brothers or sisters?

- Do you have any pets?

- When is your birthday?

- What is your favourite school subject?

- What do you like doing at the weekend?

- What did you do last weekend?

- What are you going to do next weekend?

I would choose about five, depending on the year group you are teaching, and whether you need to find out if the students can use the past or future tenses.

If you feel it is necessary, you can model the answers too:

> *Quelle est la date de ton anniversaire?* [pointing to yourself] *Mon anniversaire, c'est le 26 septembre.*

You also want this to be a short activity. The aim is to determine the students' level in the language, as well as their confidence speaking the language and participating in the lesson.

When you have completed this task, you can then begin the lesson, having a clearer idea of whom you can confidently ask for a response, who may need more support, and who may need encouragement to participate.

You can also then make a professional judgement on how much TL is appropriate in the class, how much language the students are used to hearing, and how much they are expected to use within their lessons.

Delivering the interview lesson

This may feel quite an unnatural situation, teaching students you have never met and with whom you have no rapport. You have to work through that and treat these students as you would treat those you have been working with for months in your training school.

Make sure you have at least two extra copies of your lesson plan to give to potential observers. There may be other candidates teaching a different class at the same time, and the observers may swap over mid lesson, so they can both observe both candidates.

Have a copy of your own plan to hand and make sure all of your resources are organized and laid out at the beginning of the lesson.

Once the lesson has started and you have managed to ascertain the students' level of language, you should proceed confidently with your lesson.

When the lesson finishes, remember to complete the lesson as you would normally. You may be required to dismiss the students, or you may be expected to leave the room when the lesson has finished, so that the observer can gather the students' thoughts on the lesson. It may be a good idea to confirm this before the lesson starts, so that you know how to complete the lesson effectively.

The interview day

Interviews for teaching positions are usually quite detailed processes, with several different tasks to complete during the day. You will usually find out on the day whether you have been successful or not.

There may well be several candidates being interviewed on the same day. However, on more than one occasion, I have experienced being interviewed on a separate day to others, usually owing to GCSE or A level speaking examinations. This is because many interviews happen in May, for appointments in the following September.

Usually, you will be included in a carousel of different activities. You should have a tour of the school, the interview lesson and the formal interview. A student panel may interview you, and you may also have to do some kind of written task.

Some schools may 'short-list' before the formal interview takes place; others may interview all of the candidates.

The formal interview

This normally takes between 20 and 30 minutes, but may be shorter or could run on longer, depending on whether questions are developed or not. Below is a list of possible questions. This is by no means exhaustive.

Possible questions

GENERAL QUESTIONS

- How do you think your lesson went?
- How could you improve your lesson?
- What would your next lesson look like?
- What does your classroom look like?
- If I were to enter your classroom, what would I see?
- What do you understand by the term 'differentiation'?
- Why do you want to be a teacher?
- Why do you want to work at this school?
- What skills and attributes could you bring to the school?
- Can you describe three of your strengths?
- Can you describe any of your weaknesses?
- What do you think would be your biggest challenge in the NQT year?
- Describe a lesson that you think has gone really well.
- Describe a lesson that you felt disappointed with? Why?
- What happened in the following lesson?
- Can you offer any extracurricular activities?
- What are some of the components of an outstanding lesson?
- How can you ensure student progress in every lesson?
- How can you give evidence of progress over time?

- What would you do if a student asked to talk to you to confide in you?
- What would you like to develop during your NQT year?
- What do you think of all the developments in education at the moment?
- What attracted you to this position at this school?

LANGUAGES-SPECIFIC QUESTIONS

- Can you speak any more languages than those shown on your application form?
- Would you be interested in learning a new language?
- What is your opinion about using the TL in the classroom?
- Do you have any experience in teaching EAL students?
- Would you be interested in working with EAL students? Why?
- Have you completed any cross-curricular projects during your student teaching year? How did they go? How could you help to develop cross-curricular links at this school?
- How would you go about teaching the imperfect tense/subjunctive/adjectival agreement (or other grammar structure)?
- How can you encourage students to learn their vocabulary on a regular basis and check that they have done so?
- Give an example of how you would start a lead lesson on the topic of house and home (or other topic area)?
- How do you keep up to date with French (German/Spanish/Italian) current affairs? How could you encourage A level students to keep up to date too?

Interview advice and likely questions

- How do you keep your language up to date?
- Have you any experience of observing a GCSE speaking examination?
- How would you stretch and challenge gifted linguists in your classroom?

Target language questions

Some examples in French:

- *Qu'est-ce que vous aimez faire pendant votre temps libre?*
  What do you like doing in your free time?
- *Décrivez le dernier roman que vous avez lu.*
  Describe the last book that you have read.
- *Décrivez le dernier film que vous avez vu.*
  Describe the last film that you saw.
- *Où est votre ville française préférée? Pourquoi?*
  Where is your favourite French town? Why?

Potential for A level teaching:

- *À votre avis, quel est le problème de l'environnement le plus important pour la France?*
  In your opinion, what is the biggest environmental problem for France?
- *Que pensez-vous de l'énergie nucléaire en France?*
  What do you think about nuclear energy in France?

Some examples in German:

- *Warum sollten britische Schüler eine Fremdsprache lernen?*
  Why should British pupils learn a foreign language?
- *Haben Sie in einem deutschsprachigen Land gewohnt?*
  Have you lived in a German-speaking country?
- *Was für Aktivitäten machen Spaß im Sprachunterricht?*
  What sort of activities are fun in language lessons?
- *Warum haben Sie Deutsch gelernt? Finden Sie Deutsch eine wichtige Sprache?*
  Why did you learn German? Do you think it's an important language?

You may well be interviewed in the TL. The questions could take the form of the French questions above, which are quite simplistic, or they could be more complex questions, as shown in German.

I think this was the thing that surprised me most during my first teaching interview. I wasn't prepared for it. The head of languages took his turn in the interview and immediately began speaking in French. It took me by surprise, and so I perhaps didn't perform to the best of my ability.

Therefore, be prepared to speak in the TL. If you are a dual linguist, or have a stronger or weaker language, you might be asked to teach in your second language, rather than your first one, in order for them to get an idea of how strong your weaker language is.

Student panel

More and more schools are choosing to use students in the interview process. The students may be part of a student council or student voice; they will be handpicked. Some student panels write their own questions, so be prepared to answer some interesting questions.

You should also try and have a few questions to ask the students themselves. If they are a mixture of year groups, try to ask a question of a younger student and an older one.

Some suggestions are:

- Which languages do you study? Are there any languages you would like to study?

- What are the best things about learning a language?

- If you could improve your language lessons, what would you do?

- Have you been involved in overseas trips or visits?

- Do you have opportunities to go into primary schools to support younger children in their language learning? Is this something that might interest you?

- Would you like to continue your languages studies after GCSE? Why?

A negative experience

You might not be successful at gaining the first job that you interview for. It is a tiring and wearing experience and one that, if you have interview after interview, can be very draining.

You must take something positive from an unsuccessful interview and learn from the experience. Take time to reflect on the day, what went well and those things that you feel might not have gone so well.

There is a possibility that you might feel that the job isn't the right one for you during the interview process. If you really feel strongly about that, you should try and have the courage to withdraw from the process. I have only had the courage to do this on one occasion, when the job was really not the right one for me, and I felt uncomfortable with the school's ethos.

Remember, the interview is also about you finding out whether it is the right school for you, and whether you think you would fit in there.

Feedback

As part of the process, you are entitled to feedback if you are not successful following the interview. It is highly likely that you will find out on the day whether you have been chosen for the position or not. If it is not on the day, it should be within the following few days.

It can be difficult to hear the reasons why you were not the right person for the job, particularly if you have had several interviews already.

I strongly suggest that you request feedback and that you make notes, if you feel as though it could be useful for you next time you go for an interview.

And finally

As soon as you leave the interview, note down as many questions that you were asked during the day as you can remember. When I was training, a group of us decided to exchange interview questions to support each other with interview preparation. Following every interview, I have written down the questions I can remember and the answer that I gave (if I could remember) at the time.

This really helped with reflection on my own interview technique too, as well as helping me to prepare for the next one that came along.

ACTIVITIES

1   Once you have been successful in being invited to interview, try to find time for a practice interview with your head of department. A member of the leadership team may offer this as part of your training, but it is a good idea to have a practice run.

2   When you have started to apply for jobs, think about activities that you have used in your classroom that have been successful. Think about how you could use these sorts of task in your interview lesson.

3   If you have time, you could trial a few tasks on your students, if they fit with the topic at the time.

TALKING POINTS

1   Talk to as many other student teachers as possible about your interview experiences. Swap questions that you are asked on the day. Compare tasks that you are asked to complete. In this way, you will be more prepared for the interview process.

2   What is the best interview lesson? What has gone well for any other colleagues?

3   Compare any problems that have arisen during the interview process. How can you overcome these?

4   How can you use feedback to support you in your next application, if you are not successful?

12 | Your first term in post

So, congratulations, you have successfully gained your first teaching post. Once the dust has settled, and you can see the future panning out more clearly, you will need to think about how best to organize yourself for the beginning of your first term in school.

Preparation: before you start

Some schools appoint NQTs in the July before the autumn term. This allows you, as a new teacher, to become more acquainted with your new school, new colleagues and new students. You may get to meet your new tutor group too.

The majority of schools will have a day when all of the newly appointed staff for the new term will be invited in to meet with their departments and, possibly, to meet some of their new students.

The key to a successful first term is good preparation. Use the initial visit before you start formally in the September to gather some key documents. You will need your timetable, class lists, schemes of work, a school map (if necessary) and teacher planner, and check to see if you have a school email address.

Make every effort to see your classroom, and have some time in the room if possible. Get an idea of where you will be working and imagine the kind of environment you want to create. You might take some notes of things to collect during the summer break, especially if you are going to a country where your language is spoken.

Some of the things from France I have collected over the years, which come with me from classroom to classroom, are:

- film posters bought during my year abroad;

- a world map (in French);

- a French road map of the whole country, with postcards from some of the main cities;

- pictures from some of my favourite places in France.

Once they are on the walls, I feel like it is my space, which I can then develop with other bits and pieces.

There may be space for other resources to be displayed, such as key vocabulary, definitions of grammar terms and TL phrases used in the classroom.

Remember to leave some space for student work to be displayed, once you are in post.

There may be work being carried out in the school over the holidays, and so it's a good idea to check with someone first, if you want to prepare your classroom before the summer holidays.

Either way, you can get yourself into a position so that, when you start to teach in your own classroom, it is a teaching environment that you have created and one that you feel comfortable in. Make it your own space.

Timetable

You should have your timetable made available to you before the summer holidays. Sometimes, there may be reasons why that is not possible, but your head of department should be able to tell you the classes you will be teaching and even the classes that you are likely to have on the first few days of term.

Once you have your timetable, look carefully at the classes that you are teaching and when you are teaching them. Find out if there are copies of the course book available to support your planning. Gather together your class lists and any schemes of work; ask for them if you need to.

Ask your head of department if there is a teacher planner available. Not all schools provide these, so don't assume that the school will give you one. If it does not, get yourself a teacher planner as soon as you can.

Once you have all the required information, you can start your planning for the first week of teaching.

Planning

You will need to spend some concentrated time planning; this will include planning the first lesson, and probably the first week, and having an idea of what is coming up in the first few months, perhaps the first term.

This will give you the chance to think forwards in terms of planning resources, particularly if you are going to the country where the language is spoken and you can collect some realia for your classes. Some examples of the types of realia could be:

- city maps;
- train/bus timetables;
- train/bus tickets;
- CDs of songs in the TL;
- French/German/Spanish versions of Monopoly/Scrabble/Guess Who;
- restaurant menus;
- newspaper articles;
- photographs;
- supermarket flyers showing food and drink promotions.

Chapter 7 has some ideas of how you can use these in your classroom.

You could also revisit Chapter 3 to remind yourself of where to start when planning. You may be more confident in planning your lessons now. If this is the case, do take some time to plan forward.

Try to complete some weekly plans, so you have a really good idea of what is to come over the following few months.

There will certainly be many things that might be unpredictable within your first term that you will have to deal with now you are a fully-fledged teacher. If you have some medium-term planning in place, you will find it easier to cope with those extra situations.

Expectations

You will probably work out quite quickly what the expectations are of the teachers at your school. You will need to think about what your expectations are as a result. Think about your classroom expectations: what is the level of TL expected? Is this appropriate for you and your students? Do you think that you could or would be happy to promote more TL?

Start as you mean to go on. Set your habits in the first few lessons. Be explicit about what you expect from the students. If you want them to talk to you in the TL for requests, then you need to relay that to them.

- *Je suis désolé d'être en retard.* (I'm sorry I am late.)

- *J'ai oublié mon cahier/mon livre.* (I've forgotten my book.)

- *Puis-je enlever ma veste?* (Can I take off my blazer?)

- *Puis-je aller aux toilettes?* (Can I go to the toilet?)

Make sure you know the system for rewards, as well as behaviour sanctions, so that you can be consistent with the rest of the teaching staff, and the students will know from the start that you will be following the school procedures.

Try to observe some other teachers in the department, to get an idea of what other people are doing. This is especially important in terms of TL, in particular if you are sharing groups.

It may seem like the easiest thing, but don't be afraid to ask questions. If you are not sure about something, then ask someone. It will be easier in the long run.

Extracurricular activities

At your school, there may be a culture of extracurricular activities that are run by the teachers for the students. There may well be an established French film club, a Spanish conversation group or a German theatre group that takes place each week. You may be able to support another teacher from your department with this.

If you have had some experience during your training with extracurricular clubs, you may feel more confident to run something yourself. Until you try something, you won't have any idea what the take up will be.

If you are going to create a new group, then it might be an idea to do it in the spring or summer term, rather than your first term in post. You will be in a much better position to work out the demands of the job and how much time you can realistically give to extracurricular activities.

If you are asked to join in with a different department's clubs, and you feel that it is something you would like to do, then go for it. You will get the opportunity to see the students in a different environment, and it gives you an idea of what they like doing outside the classroom.

These kinds of club really help to build relationships with students. They will give opportunities to have something else in common with the students that is not just based in the classroom.

Trips and visits

As an enthusiastic new teacher, you might well be asked if you'd like to be part of a trip or visit. This might be within your languages department, or it might be that the music department is touring in Italy and would like an Italian speaker to go too. It might be a group going on a ski trip to Austria, who would like someone who speaks German to accompany the group.

Some overseas trips are organized up to a year in advance, so don't be surprised if you are approached within your first term to be asked to accompany a trip, especially if it is abroad.

Think carefully about your other commitments and whether you would like to go. Opportunities to take students abroad don't always come up very often. Organizing trips can be a long and sometimes complex task, so you might find that the trips are biannual. Departments may well alternate between countries that they visit (France, Germany, Spain, Italy), or there may be an exchange that happens on an annual basis.

Whatever kind of trip it is, if there are no compelling reasons not to go, get involved. You will reap the benefits in the classroom and you will be able to see for yourself your students using the language that you have taught them. It doesn't get better than that.

School open day and open evening

You can guarantee that your school will have an annual open day and/or evening. It is highly likely that this will be in the first term. This is because the date of the deadline for school applications for the following year's new intake is at the end of October.

The languages department may well have a wealth of activities that it does annually to show the department at its best. Below are a few ideas of things that I have been involved in during open evenings:

- a European café – Year 7 and 8 students serving hot and cold drinks, and snacks, while speaking in the TL;
- cheese tasting and scoring in the TL;
- student books and folders available for parents to look through;
- examples of course books;
- interactive activities on the whiteboard for younger children to get involved in;

- *une chasse au trésor* (treasure hunt) through the department: clues are in pictures and TL, and there are student helpers from the school.

Make sure that you are available for the whole evening and that your classroom is full of student work on the walls for all parents to see.

Another tip is to ensure that you are ready for your lessons the following day, as it is a long day and evening, and the following day you do not want to be caught out if your lessons are not fully planned.

Parents' evenings

Parents' evenings should be placed in the school calendar so that there is a balance of when they take place, but also when the parents receive reports from the school. The first parents' evening when you are on your own may feel like a daunting prospect.

In order to be fully prepared, ensure that you know who all of your students are and that you can remember their names. This may seem a little silly, but, when you are teaching hundreds of children a week, you might have a block or confuse one child with another. It is easily done. You just have to try and prepare yourself well enough for that not to happen.

Make appointments for all the students' parents you wish to see. This is about you talking to the parents you want to see, as well as the parents talking to the teachers they want to see.

Have your class list(s) to hand, with pictures if necessary. If your school uses SIMs (or another management information system), you can print off your class list with student photographs.

Try to keep to time if possible. If the conversation is running over, then ask politely if it would be possible to make another time to continue the discussion.

Make notes for every student in your class(es). This may seem an onerous task, but you will be glad of it when the conversation runs dry, or you have something specific you want to say, or you get tired after 3 hours or so talking to parents.

It can be a long night; make sure you have a bottle of water, or accept offers of a drink during the evening.

Give the parents (and students, if they are there) specific language targets to take away with them. You may be required to do this as part of the school policy. It is good practice to do this anyway.

If you are concerned about any appointment, make sure your mentor or head of department is aware of when it is and invite them to sit in on the meeting.

If a parent doesn't turn up to the appointment, then you will need to check the sign-in list for the evening, to see if they are in school and you can find them. If not, this could be followed up with a phone call the following day.

Finally, like the open evening, parents' evening can be a long and tiring day. Make sure you are fully prepared for the next day's teaching.

Work–life balance

Your first term in post will undoubtedly be the most difficult and the most tiring term, possibly of your teaching career. The autumn term is always a long and challenging one, especially as the days become shorter, with the dark mornings and afternoons.

One way to make it easier is to remember that it is really important to try and achieve the work–life balance that you want. If you have a partner, or a family, make sure you don't forget them.

During my training year, I made a pact with myself that I would not work later than 10 p.m. If I ended up doing that, I would not be able to perform to the best of my ability the following day.

That pact still stands. In fact, it is about 9 p.m. now. Even in a leadership position, I need to rest and relax in order to be effective in the classroom, as well as in the whole-school role that I have.

It may take some time to find the right balance, but, over the first term, you should sit back and reflect on whether you think you have the right balance. If the answer is no, then consider what you can do to try and achieve it, and who you can ask if you are finding things tough.

Establishing routines

If you can set yourself a routine early on, at the beginning of your first term, you may find that this will really help you cope with the inevitable stresses and strains. Try to get into school with ample time to make sure all of your lessons are ready for the day.

If you prefer to work late and mark at school, then allow yourself some days when you do that, and some days when you go home at an earlier time.

Allow the routine to develop, and this will give you a structure to your week, your non-contact time, your teaching time, your planning and assessment time too.

Transition

There will be a transitional period of no longer being a trainee and developing into a fully-fledged teacher with your own classes. Along with that comes the accountability too. It is now your responsibility to ensure that the student books are marked, that lessons are planned, that the specification is being covered, that parents are informed if need be; the list goes on.

Don't be daunted by this. You have been trained for this position, and you should feel confident that you are able to meet the requirements to succeed.

Remember to continue to reflect on your lessons and talk openly with your NQT mentor. Be courageous and put yourself forward. Make sure you play a role in setting your own targets for the year.

The unpredictable

There will undoubtedly be times when situations occur that you will not be able to predict. That is part of working with children, and part of working in a school. You may need to be able to respond rapidly to a situation, if a child needs urgent first aid, or if there is a behaviour incident you have not had to deal with before.

In order to prepare yourself for such occasions, make sure you know where the nearest teacher is, where there is a phone, or which student you can trust to go immediately and find support. You may well need to build your resilience and find a way to cope with these difficult times.

Support

Once again, in order to cope with such situations, it is important to talk these kinds of incident through with other NQTs or your mentor or another colleague. It is likely that they will have witnessed or experienced something like it before and can support you appropriately.

Seek out other new staff and NQTs. Continue talking to one another and asking for each other's advice. Reflect on your practice too.

Fulfilment

Through the ups and downs of the first term, and perhaps the whole of the NQT year, you may need to remind yourself why you wanted to become a teacher. Remind yourself it is a vocation.

My advice: work hard, stay positive and keep smiling.

Teaching can provide you with a huge sense of fulfilment and pleasure; it can be a lot of fun, and every day is different.

It is the best job in the world.

Further reading

Buck, J. and Wightwick, C. (2013) *Teaching and Learning Languages: A Practical Guide to Learning by Doing*, Abingdon, UK: Routledge.

Cowley, S. (2010) *Getting the Buggers to Behave*, London: Continuum.

Gilbert, I. (2008) *Essential Motivation in the Classroom*, Abingdon, UK: Routledge.

Griffith, N. (2007) *100+ Ideas for Teaching Languages*, London: Continuum.

Halliwell, S., Holmes, B. and Jones, B. (2002) *You Speak, They Speak: Focus on Target Language Use*, Reading, UK: CILT.

Jones, B. and Jones, G. (2001) *Boys' Performance in Modern Foreign Languages: Listening to Learners*, Reading, UK, CILT.

Nunan, D. (1991) *Language Teaching Methodology: Textbook for Teachers*, London: Prentice Hall.

Ramage, G. (2012) *The Modern Languages Teacher's Handbook*, London: Continuum.

Rogers, B. (2012) *You Know the Fair Rule: Strategies for Positive and Effective Behaviour Management and Discipline in Schools*, Oxford, UK: Pearson.

Swan, M. (2005) *Practical English Usage*, Oxford, UK: Oxford University Press.

Turk, P. (2004) *Action Grammaire! New Advanced French Grammar*, London: Hodder Education.

Worth-Stylianou, V. (1995) *French: A Handbook of Grammar, Current Usage and Word Power*, London: Continuum.

Index

Index